Activity Book C

# VISIONS
## Language ◆ Literature ◆ Content

# Mary Lou McCloskey
# Lydia Stack

THOMSON
—✶—™
HEINLE

Australia ◇ Canada ◇ Mexico ◇ Singapore ◇ United Kingdom ◇ United States

**VISIONS ACTIVITY BOOK C**
*Mary Lou McCloskey and Lydia Stack*

**Publisher:** *Phyllis Dobbins*
**Director of Development:** *Anita Raducanu*
**Developmental Editor:** *Tania Maundrell-Brown*
**Associate Developmental Editor:** *Yeny Kim*
**Associate Developmental Editor:** *Kasia Zagorski*
**Editorial Assistant:** *Audra Longert*
**Production Supervisor:** *Mike Burggren*
**Marketing Manager:** *Jim McDonough*
**Manufacturing Manager:** *Marcia Locke*
**Director, ELL Training and Development:** *Evelyn Nelson*
**Photography Manager:** *Sheri Blaney*
**Development:** *Proof Positive/Farrowlyne Associates, Inc.; Quest Language Systems, LLC*
**Design and Production:** *Proof Positive/Farrowlyne Associates, Inc.*
**Cover Designer:** *Studio Montage*
**Printer:** *Patterson Printing*

**Cover Image:** *© George Grady Grossman/Index Stock Imagery*

Printed in the United States of America.
1 2 3 4 5 6 7 8 9 10    08  07  06  05  04  03

For more information, contact Heinle, 25 Thomson Place, Boston, Massachusetts 02210 USA, or you can visit our Internet site at http://www.heinle.com

For permission to use material from this text or product contact us:
Tel    1-800-730-2214
Fax    1-800-730-2215
Web   www.thomsonrights.com

ISBN: 0-8384-5346-5

# Contents

Name _____ Date _____

## Build Vocabulary

Use with student text page 3.

### Define Words in Context and Alphabetize

**Define Words in Context**

**Context clues** are words and sentences around a new word. The clues help you understand the meaning of the word.

She had never seen such a <u>strange</u> and unusual creature.

The word *strange* is similar in meaning to "unusual."

**A.** ➤ Read the words and definitions. Complete the sentences with the words. Use context clues to help you.

| Word and Definition | |
|---|---|
| **steep** almost straight up and down | **tiny** very small |
| **murky** unclear and dark | **high-tech** very technical; modern |
| **bulky** large | **remote** far away |

1. The _____ camera had all the latest features.

2. He could not see the fish because the water was _____.

3. The lake was in a _____ location, far away from the town.

4. He loaded the backpack with lots of food and water. It was _____.

5. The road to the lake went up a _____ mountain.

6. My dog was _____ compared to the large monster.

**Alphabetize**

The words in a dictionary are in **alphabetical order.** This makes words easy to find. These words are in alphabetical order:

**d**inosaur, **e**normous, **l**egendary, **m**onster (abc**de**fghijk**lm**nopqrstuvwxyz)

To alphabetize a group of words that begin with the same letter, look at the second letter or third letter.

s**n**ake, s**po**t, s**pr**ing s**w**arm (abcdefghijklmn**nop**qrstuv**w**xyz)

**B.** ➤ Put these words in alphabetical order. Use the second letter of each word. The first one has been done for you.

| | |
|---|---|
| creature | claim |
| apple | could |
| carrots | deep |
| challenge | |

1. _____*carrots*_____     4. _____

2. _____     5. _____

3. _____

# Writing: Punctuation

*Use with student text page 10.*

## Use Question Marks

Use a **question mark (?)** at the end of a sentence that is asking for an answer.

Where did you see the monster**?**      When did you see the monster**?**

Questions often begin with the words *how, what, who, when, where, which,* and *why.* Be careful. These words can also begin statements. End statements with a period.

When she left, she wore her red coat**.**

**A.** ➤ Edit these sentences. End questions with a question mark. End statements with a period. The first one has been done for you.

1. When scientists used a special computer, this is what they saw

   *When scientists used a special computer, this is what they saw.*
   _____

2. Which discovery amazed them

   _____

3. What did the monster look like

   _____

4. Who saw the monster's flippers

   _____

5. Where is the Loch Ness monster

   _____


**B.** ➤ Rewrite the statements as questions. Be sure to use a question mark.

1. The Loch Ness monster is in the water.

   Where _____

2. The man and the boy saw the monster.

   What _____

3. Scientists can make clear pictures.

   How _____

Name _____ Date _____

# Elements of Literature

Use with student text page 11.

## Write a Story with Visuals

**Visuals** are maps, charts, pictures, and photographs. These help readers understand a text.

**A.** ➤ Write a monster story. First, draw the monster scenes or events in order on the storyboard. Then, write the text to explain each event. Write the text on the lines.

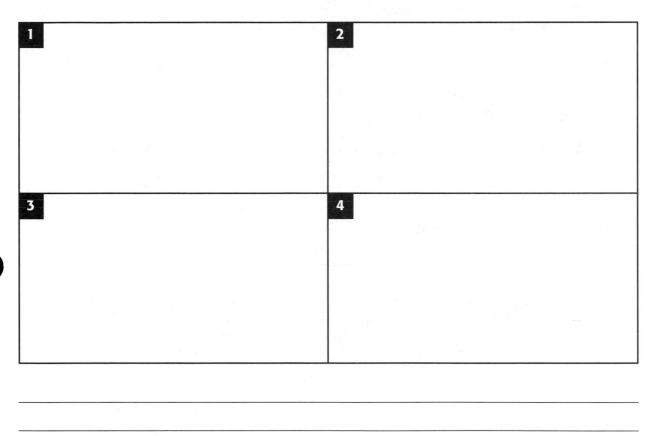

_____

_____

_____

_____

**B.** ➤ Answer these questions about your story.

**1.** What will a reader learn about your monster from the pictures? Is it tall? Is it big?

_____

**2.** What happens first in your story?

_____

**3.** How does your story end?

_____

# Word Study

*Use with student text page 12.*

## Analyze Compound Words

A **compound word** is made of two smaller words. To find the meaning of a compound word, split it into two smaller words. Then define each smaller word.

underwater

under + water → underwater

*Under* means "below or beneath."
*Water* is a liquid or body of water (such as an ocean).
*Underwater* means "beneath the surface of water."

➤ Use one word from each column to form compound words. Then write a definition for each compound word.

| | |
|---|---|
| book | shape |
| water | fall |
| news | ache |
| ear | store |
| milk | paper |

| Compound Word | Meaning |
|---|---|
| newspaper | a paper that contains news |
| | |
| | |
| | |
| | |
| | |

Name _____ Date _____

# Grammar Focus

Use with student text page 12.

## Understand the Conjunctions *But* and *And*

A **compound sentence** is two independent clauses joined together.
An **independent clause** is a sentence that can stand on its own.

Manuel and Sarah wanted to go to the park.

A compound sentence joins two independent clauses with a comma and conjunctions like *and, but,* or *or.*

Use **but** to show two different ideas.

The grandparents came to the party, but they did not stay to the end.

Use **and** to show addition.

The grandparents came to the party, and they had a great time.

**A.** ➤ Read each compound sentence. Underline the two independent clauses and circle the conjunctions. The first one has been done for you.

1. He planted crops in the field, (and) they grew very fast.

2. She worked in the town, but she did not work on the farm.

3. They worked in the store after school, and they helped at home, too.

4. He sells tomatoes in town, but he does not sell apples.

5. She sells shoes in the store, and she also sells socks.

6. They like to visit the ocean, but they do not like to visit the mountains.

**B.** ➤ Complete the sentences with *but* or *and.* The first one has been done for you.

1. I wanted to go to the soccer game, _____*but*_____ I had to stay home and rake the leaves.

2. It is usually very hot here in the summer, _____ this summer has been cool.

3. Cynthia thought the test would be hard, _____ she was right.

4. My family wanted to go to the beach this weekend, _____ it rained.

## Grammar Focus

*Use with student text page 12.*

### Use Commas with the Conjunctions *But* and *And*

Use a **comma** to join two independent clauses with conjunctions such as *but* or *and*. Put the comma before the conjunction.

It was windy yesterday**, but** today it is calm.

**A.** ➤ Read each pair of sentences. Join the two independent clauses using the conjunctions *but* or *and*. Use a comma. The first one has been done for you.

1. Everything was quiet at the lake. Then the monster came out.

   *Everything was quiet at the lake, but then the monster came out.*

2. We were scared. We ran away.

   _____

3. We ran into the woods to be safe. The woods were scary and dark.

   _____

4. We searched for the monster. We never saw it again.

   _____

5. We told other people about the monster. No one believed us.

   _____

**B.** ➤ Edit these sentences. Use commas and the words *and* and *but* correctly.

1. I wanted to go home but my friends wanted to stay.

   _____

2. It is usually cold in the winter but, this winter has been warm.

   _____

3. My father wants to swim in the lake, and the water is murky.

   _____

Name _____  Date _____

## From Reading to Writing

*Use with student text page 13.*

### Edit a Paragraph that Describes

➤ Use the checklist to edit the paragraph you wrote in Chapter 1.

**Editing Checklist for a Paragraph that Describes**

Title of paragraph: _____

**What I did:**

_____ **1.** I reviewed the reading selection to get ideas.

_____ **2.** I looked at paragraphs 3, 11, and 13 and used them as models for my writing.

_____ **3.** I looked at the visuals in the reading selection to get ideas.

_____ **4.** I drew a picture of the Loch Ness monster.

_____ **5.** I wrote my descriptive paragraph under my picture.

_____ **6.** I used descriptive words such as *enormous* and *ferocious*.

_____ **7.** I used a dictionary to check the spellings of difficult words.

_____ **8.** I indented my paragraph.

## Across Content Areas

*Use with student text page 13.*

### Use Media Resources for Research

Use **audio-visual resources** for research for reports.

**Audio resources** include CD-ROMs, audio cassettes, and CDs. The Internet also can be used as an audio resource. Use these resources to hear sounds and listen to information about a subject.

**Visual resources** include maps, photographs, drawings, video, and the Internet. CD-ROMs also have pictures and video. Use these resources to see images and moving pictures about a subject.

a drawing          an audio CD        a video          a CD-ROM          a map          the Internet
or                 or an
a photograph       audio cassette

➤ Tell how you would use each resource to add interest to a report about the Loch Ness monster. Complete each sentence. Use the words above.

1. If I want to show where Loch Ness is, I can use _____.

2. If I want to play a song about the monster, I can use

    _____ or _____.

3. If I want to show an animal from my imagination, I can make

    _____.

4. If I want to show moving pictures of the search for the monster, I

    can use _____.

5. If I want to show pictures about Loch Ness, I can find some on

    _____ or on _____.

# Build Vocabulary

*Use with student text page 15.*

## Use Headwords to Locate Synonyms

The **head words** in a dictionary are the words that are being defined. They are at the beginning of the entry, and they are in dark (bold) type. They are in alphabetical order.

head word ——— | **act** /ækt/ *verb* to behave or show: *She acted happy.*

**A.** ➤ Write the head word for each of these definitions.

**modern** /ˈmɑdərn/ *adjective*
belonging to the present time, new

1. _____

**region** /ˈridʒən/ *noun* an area of a country, territory

2. _____

**symbolize** /ˈsɪmbəˌlaiz/ *verb* to be a symbol of, embody

3. _____

A synonym is a word that has a meaning similar to another word. For example, *huge* is a synonym for *large.* You can often find synonyms in dictionary entries.

**B.** ➤ Use the dictionary entries above to answer the questions.

1. What is a synonym for *region?* _____
2. What is a synonym for *symbolize?* _____
3. What is a synonym for *modern?* _____

# Writing: Capitalization

Use with student text page 22.

## Capitalize Proper Nouns

A **proper noun** is a particular person, place, or thing.
Capitalize the names of particular people, places, and things.

| Capitalize Proper Nouns | |
|---|---|
| people | Selena Hernandez<br>Helena Boxer |
| places | Mississippi River<br>Texas |
| things | Olympics<br>October |

➤ Edit these sentences. Find the proper nouns. Capitalize the names of particular people, places, and things.

1. The navajo called them ancient enemies.

   _____

2. These people settled in colorado.

   _____

3. Katherine lives in durango, colorado.

   _____

4. The cliff dwellings of mesa verde were abandoned.

   _____

5. The pueblo indians live in arizona and new mexico.

   _____

6. leighana sisneros and landon wigton went with her.

   _____

VISIONS C Activity Book • Copyright © Heinle

# Elements of Literature

*Use with student text page 23.*

## Identify the Speaker and Write Quotes

Writers use **quotes** to tell the reader exactly what a character says. **Quotation marks** (" . . . ") show the reader that there is a quote. Look at the following examples of quotations:

"I went to the park to play with my dog," says Michael.

Maria said, "I wanted to go to the park, but I was too busy."

Put quotation marks around the words that the characters speak. Put commas inside the quotation marks to set off the quote from the speaker of the quote.

**A.** ➤ Rewrite the sentences by placing quotation marks around the quotes. The first one has been done for you.

**1.** I can't go to the movie, Lisa said.

*"I can't go to the movie," Lisa said.* _____

**2.** Thomas said, I think it is going to be a very good movie.

_____

**3.** I have to clean my room before lunch, said Lisa.

_____

**4.** If I help you clean, we can see the movie, Thomas said.

_____

**5.** Lisa said, Let's get started.

_____

Writers use quotes as a way "to show" not simply "tell" the action of a story.

**B.** ➤ Read the first paragraph. Then complete the second paragraph. Include quotes to "show" rather than "tell" the action or events.

A girl goes to the ruins with two other people. They admire the ancient people. The boy knows about the religious events. The girl has ideas about why the ancient people moved away from the cliffs.

A ten-year-old girl visits the ruins with two other children. She admires the ancient people. She says," _____." Her friends have ideas about the people, too. The boy says, " _____." The girl says, " _____."

# Word Study

*Use with student text page 24.*

## Study Root Words and Suffixes

The suffix *-ist* changes a word to a noun. It tells what a person does.
If the word ends in *y*, drop the *y* and then add *-ist*.

geology → -ist = geologist

**A.** ➤ Fill in the chart. Use a dictionary to fill in the definitions.

| Word | Suffix | New Word | Meaning |
|------|--------|----------|---------|
| archaeology | | | |
| geology | -ist | | |
| biology | | | |
| guitar | | | |

**B.** ➤ Complete these sentences with a new word from the chart.

1. My brother is a _____ in a rock band.

2. I'm thinking about becoming an _____ because I like ancient cultures.

3. A _____ can explain how earthquakes happen.

4. A _____ studies living things.

Name _____    Date _____

# Grammar Focus

Use with student text page 24.

## Use Prepositional Phrases of Place

A **preposition** is a part of speech. It can tell *where* something is.

The paper is <u>on</u> the desk.

| Common Prepositions of Place | | | | |
|---|---|---|---|---|
| above<br>across<br>around<br>at | behind<br>between<br>down<br>from | in<br>into<br>near<br>on | onto<br>out<br>through<br>to | under<br>up<br>upon<br>with |

A **prepositional phrase** is a group of words that begins with a preposition and ends with a noun or pronoun.

The soccer game is <u>at the park</u>.

My dinner is <u>on the table</u>.

**A.** ➤ Underline the prepositional phrase in each sentence. The first one has been done for you.

**1.** Jerry's money is <u>at the bank</u>.

**2.** My letters are in the mailbox.

**3.** Kara and Lindsey are at the beach.

**4.** The lion is sleeping on the large rock.

**5.** All the snacks are in the jar.

**6.** My homework is on my desk.

**B.** ➤ Look at the prepositional phrases you underlined above. Complete a question for each phrase using the word *where*. The first one has been done for you.

**1.** Where is ___*Jerry's money*___?

**2.** Where are _____?

**3.** Where are _____?

**4.** Where is _____?

**5.** Where are _____?

**6.** Where is _____?

# Grammar Focus

*Use with student text page 24.*

## Write Prepositional Phrases

Writers develop or improve their ideas by using prepositional phrases. Look at the following example:

I parked the car.

I parked the car <u>near the store</u>.

Adding the prepositional phrase "near the store" improves the sentence because it elaborates on the idea.

➤ Elaborate the written idea in each sentence. Add a prepositional phrase from the box to each sentence. Write a new sentence. The first one has been done for you.

| | |
|---|---|
| in the cliffs | on top of the mesa |
| in the region | in pottery |
| from Durango | |

1. The Pueblo people built huge homes.

   *The Pueblo people built huge homes in the cliffs.*

2. The women cooked corn.

   _____

3. The men planted corn.

   _____

4. Little rain fell.

   _____

5. Katherine visited the ruins with her friends.

   _____

Student
Handbook

Name _____ Date _____

# From Reading to Writing

*Use with student text page 25.*

## Edit an Informational Text

➤ Use the checklist to edit the informational text you wrote in Chapter 2.

**Editing Checklist for an Informational Text**

Title of informational text: _____

**What I did:**

_____ 1. I described what the place looked like.

_____ 2. I wrote about the number of people who lived there.

_____ 3. I used prepositional phrases to tell when and where something happened.

_____ 4. I described how the people lived.

_____ 5. I indented my paragraph.

_____ 6. I proofread my paper to check for spelling, capitalization, and grammar errors.

_____ 7. I created a final draft of my paragraph.

## Across Content Areas

*Use with student text page 25.*

### Compare Texts

Read this encyclopedia article about the Anasazi. Compare this article with the information in "Mystery of the Cliff Dwellers" in your textbook.

**The Appearance of the Anasazi**

Where did the Anasazi come from? Why did they make Mesa Verde their home? Scientists are not sure. They know that in A.D. 440 a few small groups of Anasazi climbed the mesa. The Anasazi made their homes in the caves on the sides of the cliffs.

**The Disappearance of the Anasazi**

For a long time, the Anasazi lived in the cliffs. In 1276, a **drought**, or dry period, began. There was no rain. The people of the Southwest had little water. Corn crops did not grow without water. Many of the Anasazi left the cliff dwellings because there was no water or food. By 1300, all the people had left.

Scientists have some ideas about what the Anasazi did next. When they left Mesa Verde, they may have joined the Pueblo groups. These groups lived in Arizona and New Mexico.

**A.** ➤ Use a Venn Diagram to compare and contrast the information in the text above with "Mystery of the Cliff Dwellers."

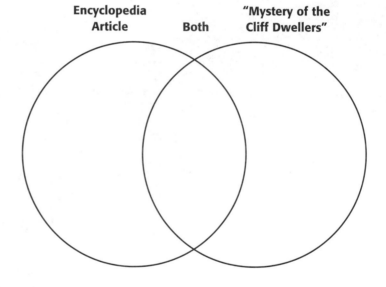

Encyclopedia Article   Both   "Mystery of the Cliff Dwellers"

**B.** ➤ Answer the questions. Use the Venn Diagram.

1. In the encyclopedia article, when did the Anasazi first appear in Mesa Verde?

_____

2. In "Mystery of the Cliff Dwellers," when did the Anasazi first appear in Mesa Verde?

_____

3. In the encyclopedia article, why did the Anasazi leave and disappear?

_____

4. In "Mystery of the Cliff Dwellers," why did the Anasazi leave and disappear?

_____

5. What information did you find in both texts?

_____

VISIONS Unit 1 • Chapter 2 Mystery of the Cliff Dwellers

VISIONS C Activity Book • Copyright © Heinle

# Build Vocabulary

Use with student text page 27.

## Understand Dictionaries

A dictionary entry tells you more than the meanings of words. Look at the entry below.

Pronunciation   Part of Speech

Definition

Entry Word
(guide word)

**diary** /daɪəri/ *noun* a written record of a person's feelings, thoughts, and activities: *He wrote about each day in his diary.*

**A.** ➤ Fill in the chart. Use the dictionary entry above and the ones below to get the information.

| Word | Part of Speech | Definition |
|------|----------------|------------|
| diary | | |
| wrist | | |
| eardrum | | |
| blood | | |

**blood** /blʌd/ *noun* the red liquid pumped by the heart through the body

**eardrum** /ˈɪrˌdrʌm/ *noun* the part inside the ear that moves so that one can hear sound

**wrist** /rɪst/ *noun* the joint attaching the hand to the forearm

**B.** ➤ Write a sentence for each of the words in the chart.

1. _____

2. _____

3. _____

4. _____

# Writing: Spelling

*Use with student text page 34.*

## Form Plurals

Most words in English form plurals by adding -*s* or -*es* to the end of a word.

➤ Study the rules. Then complete the chart.

| Some Rules for Plurals | | |
|---|---|---|
| **Noun Ends in** | **General Rule** | **Examples** |
| **1.** Consonants and Vowels | Add -*s* | eyebrow → eyebrows <br> drum → _____ <br> book → _____ <br> heartbeat → _____ <br> muscle → _____ |
| **2.** *ch* <br> *s* <br> *sh* <br> *x* <br> *z* | Add -*es* | watch → watches <br> toss → tosses <br> brush → _____ <br> ax → axes <br> buzz → _____ |
| **3.** Consonant + *y* | Change *y* to *i* <br> Add -*es* | baby → babies <br> diary → _____ |
| **4.** Vowel + *o* | Add -*s* | video → videos <br> rodeo → _____ |

# Elements of Literature

*Use with student text page 35.*

**Use the Pronoun *You***

An author uses **direct address** by writing to the reader using the pronoun *you*. Direct address is often used in giving instructions.

➤ Answer each question. Write sentences. Use second person by using the pronoun *you*.

1. How do you make a peanut butter and jelly sandwich?

   *First, you need to get two pieces of bread. Then you should spread peanut butter on one side of the bread.*

   *Next, you should choose your favorite jelly. Spread the jelly on evenly. Put the two pieces of bread together.*

   *Now you have your peanut butter and jelly sandwich.*

2. How do you make a bed?

   _____

   _____

   _____

3. How do you change the batteries in a CD player?

   _____

   _____

   _____

   _____

4. How do you _____? (You decide on the topic.)

   _____

   _____

   _____

# Word Study

*Use with student text page 36.*

## Write Using Contractions

**Contractions** are used in informal speech and writing to make words shorter. They are formed by joining two words together. Letters are dropped from one of the words and replaced by an apostrophe (').

Today <u>has not</u> been very cold.

Today <u>hasn't</u> been very cold.

| Word | Word | Contraction |
|------|------|-------------|
| you | are | you're |
| it | is | it's |
| what | is | what's |
| they | will | they'll |
| did | not | didn't |

**A.** ➤ Rewrite the sentences with contractions.

1. You are tired.

_____

2. It is just a yawn.

_____

3. What is the purpose of yawning?

_____

4. You are bored or sleepy.

_____

5. They will be sleepy.

_____

6. He did not stop there.

_____

7. They will yawn when they stretch.

_____

8. They did not yawn.

_____

Name _____ Date _____

# Grammar Focus

Use with student text page 36.

## Write Dependent Clauses

A **dependent clause** has a subject and a verb, but is not a complete sentence. It cannot stand alone.

A dependent clause often begins with the word *that*.

I explained <u>that I missed my bus.</u>

A **main clause** (or **independent clause**) has a subject and a verb. It is a complete sentence. It can stand alone.

<u>I explained</u> that I missed my bus.

**A.** ➤ Complete the sentences by adding a dependent clause starting with *that*.

1. My mother and father think _that I should help my grandmother._____

2. You said _____.

3. My brother told me _____.

4. My teacher told the class _____.

5. After the game, the coach said _____.

6. Please tell your sister _____.

**B.** ➤ Complete the sentences by adding a main clause.

1. _____ that I will take my brother with me.

   _I think that I will take my brother with me._____

2. _____ that they want me to join the club.

   _____

3. _____ that she is going to China.

   _____

4. _____ that she forgot to tell us about the party.

   _____

5. _____ that I need a ride to the mall.

   _____

# Grammar Focus

*Use with student text page 36.*

## Write Complex Sentences

A **complex sentence** contains an independent clause (or main clause) and one or more dependent clauses.

```
        independent          dependent
          clause              clause
        ⌐I think⌐⌐that I will do well on the test.⌐
```

**A.** ➤ Combine the clauses in the chart to form five complex sentences. Write in complete sentences.

| | |
|---|---|
| Sarah knows | that the Rangers are the best team |
| They understand | that he forgot to do his homework |
| Manuel realizes | that the story is exciting |
| Juan believes | that one plus one equals two |
| | that they must do their homework |

1. *Juan believes that the Rangers are the best team.* _____

2. _____

3. _____

4. _____

5. _____

Student
Handbook

Name _____  Date _____

# From Reading to Writing
## Write a Paragraph Using Chronology

*Use with student text page 37.*

➤ Use the checklist to edit the informational text you wrote in Chapter 3.

**Editing Checklist for a Paragraph Using Chronology**

Title of paragraph: _____

**What I did:**

_____ **1.** My paragraph is about my morning routine.

_____ **2.** I started my paragraph with a sentence telling what the paragraph will be about.

_____ **3.** I used time words such as *first, then, next,* and *last* to show chronology.

_____ **4.** I wrote at least one sentence with a dependent clause beginning with *that*.

_____ **5.** I used the writing model in my textbook.

## Across Content Areas

*Use with student text page 37.*

### Use a Bar Graph

A **bar graph** is a graph with bars of different lengths. To get information from the graph, look at the side of the graph, the bottom, and the bars.

➤ Answer the questions. Use the bar graph about watching videos.

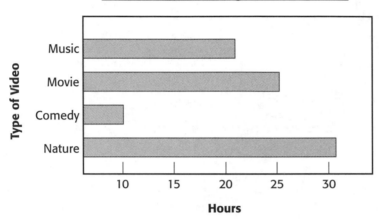

**Sam's Video Viewing Over 4 Months**

1. How many hours of music did Sam view?

   _____

2. How many hours of movies did Sam view?

   _____

3. How many hours of nature videos did Sam view?

   _____

4. How many hours of comedy videos did Sam view?

   _____

5. Which type of video did Sam watch the most?

   _____

# Build Vocabulary

## Choose Definitions

Many words in dictionaries have more than one meaning.

This entry has three definitions or meanings for the word *mystery*. Look at the numbers **(1, 2, 3)** in the entry.

> **mystery** /ˈmɪstəri/ *noun* **1** an event that has no known cause: *The robbery is still a mystery.* **2** a secret: *The package is a mystery to me.* **3** a story that includes a character who commits a crime: *My brother is reading a mystery.*

If a dictionary gives more than one definition for a word, choose the one that fits the **context.**

Context is the words and sentences that surround a specific word.

➤ Read each sentence and the definitions. Choose the correct definition of the underlined word based on the context.

1. He decided to take a <u>taxi</u> to the restaurant.
   **a.** a car that people hire to take them places
   **b.** slow movement of an airplane

2. The police officer gave the students some <u>pointers</u> on how to solve a crime.
   **a.** pieces of advice
   **b.** long sticks used to point things out on a wall map

3. The clerk was not sure what to <u>charge</u> for the coat.
   **a.** set as the price
   **b.** accuse
   **c.** attack

4. The inspector wanted to <u>check</u> the contents in the briefcase.
   **a.** a written statement of the amount due in a restaurant
   **b.** examine

# Writing: Punctuation

Use with student text page 46.

## Punctuate Dialogue

**Dialogue** is the exact words that characters say. Dialogue is shown by placing quotation marks (**"...")** around the words that are spoken.

| Rules for Punctuating Dialogue | |
|---|---|
| **Rules** | **Examples** |
| Quotation marks always appear in pairs. They are placed before the first word said and after the last word said. | "That's easy to explain," said Mr. Fink |
| Periods, commas, question marks, and exclamation points are always placed inside quotation marks. | "I'm sure he won't be happy," said the inspector. |
| Use a comma to set off words of direct address. | "What's the matter, Miguel?" |

➤ Rewrite and correct the sentences by placing quotation marks around the dialogue. Use the chart to help you.

1. Mr. Fink rubbed his chin. This isn't the briefcase I handed over to the checkroom, he said.

   _____

2. The Inspector said, you told us it was yours. You said it contained only a couple of magazines.

   _____

3. Lucky you, said the Inspector.

   _____

4. I don't mind at all, said Mr. Fink. I've got nothing to hide he said.

   _____

VISIONS C Activity Book • Copyright © Heinle

Name _____ Date _____

# Elements of Literature

Use with student text page 47.

## Evaluate Plot

The order of events in a story is called the **plot.**

**Background** is usually at the beginning. It includes information about the characters and setting. The conflict or problem is often presented in the beginning of the story.

**Rising action** is when the suspense builds.

**Climax** is the point of greatest suspense in a story.

**Resolution** is when the story comes to a close.

**A.** ➤ Read the story. Complete the chart to show the parts of the plot.

**Mystery Woman**

The policewoman waited in her car. She saw a woman run out of a store. The woman was carrying a package. The woman got into her car. She drove away. The policewoman followed her. The woman was driving very fast. The policewoman put on her lights. She told the woman to pull over. The policewoman noticed the package. She asked the woman what was in it. The woman said she had bought baby medicine. Her baby was sick at home with her husband. The policewoman told her not to drive too fast. The woman went home.

| Background | Rising Action | Climax | Resolution |
|---|---|---|---|
|  |  |  |  |

**B.** ➤ Answer the questions. Use the chart.

1. How many characters are in the story? Who are they?

_____

2. What action or event sets up the background?

_____

3. At first, what did you think the woman did in the store?

_____

4. How did the events come to a close?

_____

# Word Study

*Use with student text page 48.*

## Use -th in Numbers

**Cardinal numbers** are numbers that show amount.

*two, thirty,* and *ninety-seven.*

My family has <u>two</u> dogs.

**Ordinal numbers** are numbers that show order.

*first, eleventh,* and *twenty-fifth.*

Most ordinal numbers are formed by adding *-th* to the cardinal number.

*four**th**, seventeen**th**,* and *twenty-seven**th***

Ordinal numbers from twenty to ninety that end in *y* are formed by changing the *y* to an *i* and adding *-eth.*

twent**ieth**, thirt**ieth**, fort**ieth**, fift**ieth**

Exceptions are:

one—**first**

two—**second**

three—**third**

➤ Write the ordinal number next to the cardinal number listed. The first one has been done for you.

1. twenty, _____*twentieth*_____

2. four, _____

3. sixty, _____

4. forty-six, _____

5. seven, _____

6. ninety, _____

7. sixty-six, _____

8. seventy, _____

## Grammar Focus

*Use with student text page 48.*

### Identify Simple, Compound, and Complex Sentences

➤ Study the chart to find out what makes **simple, compound,** and **complex sentences.**

| | Definition | Example |
|---|---|---|
| **Simple Sentence** | an independent clause that can stand alone as a sentence | "The Sneak Thief" is a mystery. |
| **Compound Sentence** | more than one independent clause; is joined by a comma and a conjunction such as *or, but,* or *and* | Mary wants to go to the play, but I want to go to the baseball game. |
| **Complex Sentence** | an independent clause and one or more dependent clauses joined by a conjunction such as *when* or *although* | Although I like doughnuts, I think I will have a piece of fruit instead. |

**A.** ➤ Read the sentences. Write *simple, compound,* or *complex.*

1. _____*simple*_____ She likes baseball.

2. _____ She wants to play guitar, and he wants to play the piano.

3. _____ Harry thinks that his hard work will be rewarded.

4. _____ Because you were late, you missed the beginning of the movie.

5. _____ He is very smart.

**B.** ➤ Use each word to write a compound or complex sentence. Write in complete sentences. Then write if the sentence is *compound* or *complex.*

**1.** but

_____

**2.** that

_____

**3.** because

_____

**4.** and

_____

Name _____ Date _____

# Grammar Focus

*Use with student text page 48.*

## Punctuate Compound and Complex Sentences

**Punctuation Rules for Compound and Complex Sentences**

| Sentence | Rule | Example |
|---|---|---|
| **Compound sentence** | Use a **comma (,)** before *and, but,* or any conjunction that joins the main clauses of a compound sentence. | Mary wants to go to the play, but I want to go to the baseball game. |
| **Complex sentence** | If the dependent clause comes first, set off with a comma. | Although I like pizza, I will have a piece of fruit instead.<br><br>Some people think that yawning is caused by boredom. |

➤ Edit these sentences. Use the correct punctuation and rewrite each sentence. The first one has been done for you.

1. Bansi is going to the dance or she is going to the movie.

   *Bansi is going to the dance, or she is going to the movie.*

2. Although, she is a singer she gets nervous on stage.

   _____

3. The story, that the teacher read in class, was a mystery.

   _____

4. I would like to play soccer today but, I have to help my brother.

   _____

5. I will take out the garbage, when the rain stops.

   _____

Student Handbook

VISIONS C  Activity Book • Copyright © Heinle

Name _____  Date _____

# From Reading to Writing
## Prewrite Using a Story Map

*Use with student text page 49.*

A story map can help you understand a story. It can also be used to organize your thoughts before you write.

**A.** ➤ Think of a story and fill in the story map.

| Story Map of _____  by _____ |
|---|
| **Story Elements** |
| Characters: |
| Setting: |
| First event: |
| Reaction: |
| Problem: |
| Attempt to resolve problem: |
| Resolution of problem: |
| Resolution: |

**B.** ➤ Write your story. Use the story map in Activity A.

_____

_____

_____

_____

_____

_____

_____

## Across Content Areas

Use with student text page 49.

### Use an Index

An index is a list of subjects in alphabetical order. It gives page numbers. An index is found in the back of a book. Many informational books have an index.

**Topics** are listed in alphabetical order —

**Badlands National Park,** 42–61, 78, 115, 178–179

**Black Hills Gold Rush,** 19–27, 43, 127

**Black Hills National Forest,** 20–22, 58–60, 152

**Crazy Horse National Monument,** 122–127, 130, 132–135

**Deadwood,** 145–146
    **mining of,** 146
    **tourism,** 145–146

**Related details** are often listed for a topic.

**Page numbers** show you where to find the information.

➤ Answer the questions. Use the index.

1. On which pages can you find information about the Black Hills Gold Rush?

    _____

2. On which page can you find information about mining in the town of Deadwood, South Dakota?

    _____

3. If you looked on page 130, what topic would you be reading about?

    _____

4. Would the entry for Mount Rushmore be located before or after Badlands National Park?

    _____

Name _____ Date _____

# Build Vocabulary

*Use with student text page 51.*

## Recognize Homonyms

**Homonyms** are words that are pronounced and spelled the same, but have different meanings.

*Weight* and *wait* sound the same.

*Weight* means "the measure of something or something heavy."

*Wait* means "to stay."

## Choose the Correct Homonym

➤ Underline the correct homonym in each sentence. Then rewrite each sentence. Use your dictionary to help you. The first one has been done for you.

1. The people of Sleepy Hollow tell (tails/<u>tales</u>).

   *The people of Sleepy Hollow tell tales.*
   _____

2. People think he rides out (to/too/two) look for his missing head.

   _____

3. Ichabod Crane was (won/one) of the men who listened to these stories.

   _____

4. Ichabod's head looks like a weather (vane/vein/vain) pointing in the direction of the wind.

   _____

5. Ichabod (would/wood) help with chores around the farms.

   _____

6. He (made/maid) the choice to listen to the scary stories.

   _____

# Writing: Punctuation

*Use with student text page 60.*

## Use Commas in a Series

**Commas** are used to separate items in a **series.** A series is a list of three or more items.

I will buy <u>eggs</u>, <u>milk</u>, and <u>bananas</u> at the grocery store.

I will make *a shirt*, *a dress*, or *a coat*.

Use the conjunction *and* or *or* before the last item in the series. Put commas after each item except the last.

**A.** ➤ Edit these sentences. Rewrite each sentence adding the missing commas. The first one has been done for you.

1. I want to watch a drama a comedy or an adventure.

   *I want to watch a drama, a comedy, or an adventure.*

2. Before the first day of school, I bought pens pencils and paper.

   _____

3. My mother is cooking chicken potatoes and corn for dinner.

   _____

4. We will paint the house white green yellow or blue.

   _____

**B.** ➤ Complete the sentences. Use the word box. Include commas in a series and the conjunction *and* or *or*.

| | | | |
|---|---|---|---|
| oranges | paper | a dog | poems |
| lemons | paint | a cat | plays |
| bananas | brushes | a bird | novels |

1. I take care of _____.

2. We picked _____.

3. She writes _____.

4. He makes art with _____.

VISIONS C Activity Book • Copyright © Heinle

Name _____ Date _____

# Elements of Literature

*Use with student text page 61.*

## Analyze Setting and Tone

The **setting** is the time and place of a story. "The Legend of Sleepy Hollow" takes place in a town in New York after the Revolutionary War.

**Tone** is the way an author writes that suggests the author's feelings about a character or part of the story. The tone can be funny, angry, scary, or sad.

**A.** ➤ Match the setting to the correct plot.

### Setting: Place and Time

_____a_____ **1.** a school auditorium in the present

_____ **2.** an island in the Pacific Ocean in 1900

_____ **3.** a village in Massachusetts in November, 1621

_____ **4.** somewhere in California in 1849

_____ **5.** a frozen place near the North Pole at any time

### Plot

**a.** Two 12-year-olds compete in the finals of a spelling contest. The year is 2003.

**b.** A group of miners, called *forty-niners,* celebrate after finding gold.

**c.** Native Americans and English settlers celebrate the first Thanksgiving.

**d.** A pair of polar bears search for their lost cubs.

**e.** After a shipwreck, sailors swim to shore and try to make a plan to return home.

**B.** ➤ Write a sentence to show each tone. Use dialogue or narrative.

**1.** anger

*She stomped away after her dog ruined her favorite shoes.*

**2.** happiness

_____

**3.** humor; something funny

_____

**4.** sympathy (compassion or comfort)

_____

# Word Study

*Use with student text page 62.*

### Analyze the Suffix *-less*

The suffix *-less* means "without." When *-less* is added to a noun, the new word becomes an **adjective.** An adjective is a word that describes a noun.

head + -less → headless

**A. ➤** Fill in the chart. Add *-less* to each base word. Then write the definition of each adjective. Use your dictionary to help you.

| Noun | Suffix | New Word (Adjective) | Meaning |
|------|--------|----------------------|---------|
| 1. flavor | -less | | |
| 2. worth | -less | | |
| 3. meaning | -less | | |
| 4. help | -less | | |
| 5. humor | -less | | |
| 6. effort | -less | | |

**B. ➤** Complete the sentences. Use the adjectives from the chart.

1. He is not very funny. He is _____.

2. This food is _____. I don't like it.

3. My stereo is broken. It is _____.

4. That sentence does not have a verb. It is _____.

5. She is not helpful in the kitchen. She is _____ at making dinner.

6. He makes cooking look so easy. He makes it look _____.

# Grammar Focus

*Use with student text page 62.*

## Recognize and Use Pronoun Referents

A **pronoun** is a word that takes the place of a noun. *She, he, her, him, me,* and *it* are all examples of pronouns. A **pronoun referent** is the noun that the pronoun replaces. The pronoun *refers* to the noun.

Pablo enjoys playing soccer. He is a very good soccer player.

*Pablo* is the pronoun referent for the pronoun *He. He* refers to Pablo.

➤ Underline the pronoun referent in the first sentence. Circle the pronoun in the second sentence.

1. Jane folded the paper and placed it in a drawer. She is very organized.

2. The girls like karate. They practice twice a day.

3. Ferdinand and I walk to the park. We like to walk together.

4. The machine is fixed. It is very nice now.

5. Thomas, Miguel, and Marsha went to the zoo. They had a good time.

6. Ichabod is not lazy. He works for farmers.

7. Ichabod eats a lot. He is always hungry.

8. The story is scary. I like it.

Name _____  Date _____

# Grammar Focus

*Use with student text page 62.*

## Use Subject and Object Pronouns

A **subject pronoun** is a pronoun that is the subject of a sentence. The subject is the noun that performs the action. *I, you, he, she, it, we,* and *they* are subject pronouns.

An **object pronoun** comes after a verb or words like from, *for,* or *to. Me, you, him, her, it, us,* and *them* are object pronouns.

|  | Subject Pronouns | Object Pronouns |
|---|---|---|
| **One Person** | I, you, he, she, it | Me, you, him, her, it |
| **Examples** | I wrote it.<br>She read it. | She ate it.<br>I wrote it. |
| **More than One Person** | We, you, they | Us, you, them |
| **Examples** | They like it.<br>We ate it. | We ate them.<br>We read them. |

**A.** ➤ Complete each sentence with the correct pronouns.

1. Pablo gave a present to Maria. _____*He*_____ gave the present to _____*her*_____ yesterday.

2. My father painted the house. _____ made _____ look very nice.

3. My mother made cookies for the students. _____ also made brownies for _____ .

4. My friends are playing the stereo. _____ are playing _____ too loudly.

**B.** ➤ Write a new sentence using subject and object pronouns.

1. James likes action movies.
   *He likes them.*

2. Marcos and Uneza enjoy video games.

3. Ryan studies math every night.

4. The tree lost its leaves.

VISIONS C  Activity Book • Copyright © Heinle

Name _____  Date _____

# From Reading to Writing

*Use with student text page 63.*

## Write a Paragraph Using Hyperbole

**Hyperbole** is exaggeration for emphasis or humor. To exaggerate means to say something is more important, better, bigger, smaller, or worse than it really is.

Hyperbole often adds to the tone of a story. The **tone** is the author's attitude about the story.

Hyperbole: His hands <u>dangled a mile out of his sleeves.</u> (they were long)

Hyperbole: His <u>feet are shovels.</u> (they were big)

**A.** ➤ Rewrite each sentence. Use hyperbole and the word box.

| | |
|---|---|
| is a bucket of snakes | is sweet perfume |
| is 50 feet long | are as tall as mountains |

1. The garden is filled with flowers.

_____

2. That fish is big.

_____

3. Her hair is messy.

_____

4. The waves are high.

_____

**B.** ➤ Write a description of the Headless Horseman. Use hyperbole for each item in the list. Put your new descriptions in the web.

| | |
|---|---|
| He is dark. | He is angry. |
| He is unusual. | He is wearing a coat. |

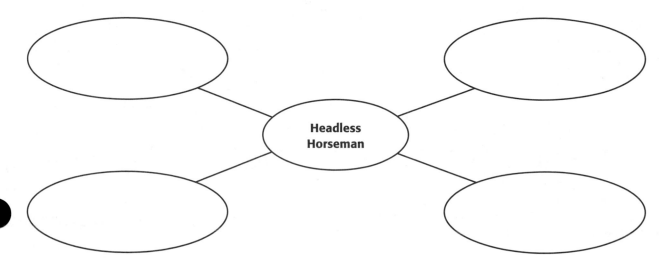

## Across Content Areas

*Use with student text page 63.*

### Research Using Note Cards

**Notes** are important words and ideas that you write down as you do research. The notes help you organize information from your research.

Use **note cards** to record information.

Use your own words.

Use quotation marks when you copy exactly what you read in the research.

➤ Read the biography of Washington Irving. Record notes on the cards.

**Washington Irving**

**Early life**

Washington Irving was born in New York City in 1783. He wanted to be a writer when he was a teenager. He wrote for a newspaper. Then he became a lawyer. He wanted to be a writer again. He wrote a few books about New York. His early books made fun of people who lived in New York.

**Life in Europe**

Irving helped with his family's business in 1810. He moved to England in 1815 to help work in the business there. After the business failed, Irving wrote books again. He still lived in England. He wrote stories and short works about the United States and England. He wrote two important stories at this time, "Rip Van Winkle" and "The Legend of Sleepy Hollow." He stayed in Europe until 1832.

**Back in New York**

In 1832, Irving returned to New York. He visited the American West. He wrote history and biographies later in life. He died in 1859.

Source: Montana, Jack. *Biography of Washington Irving*. Sleepy Hollow Books. New York, NY. 2003.

```
Research Question: What did Washington Irving do
for a living?

Notes:

Quotes:

Source:

```

# Build Vocabulary

*Use with student text page 73.*

## Define Words in Context

Context clues are words and sentences that surround a specific word. They help you understand the meaning of the word.

Everyone was <u>excited</u> about the party. Andrew was really *enthusiastic* about it. It would be his <u>first party</u> at the new school.

The clues *excited* and *first party* help you understand that *enthusiastic* means "very interested in something."

### Define Words in Context

A. ➤ Match the underlined word in each sentence to its definition.

**Word in a Sentence**

1. ___*f*___ I could not see clearly in the bright sunlight. Objects seemed to <u>blur</u>.

2. _____ I was <u>momentarily</u> confused, but I soon remembered her name.

3. _____ The coach's eyes narrowed as he <u>glared</u> at his losing team.

4. _____ I had a <u>severe</u> pain in my hand after I fell on the ice.

5. _____ I dropped the vase, but I was happy to see that it was still <u>intact</u>.

**Definition**

a. very serious

b. for a short time

c. looked at in an angry way

d. in one piece; not broken

e. make it harder to see clearly

### Write Words in Context

B. ➤ Write a sentence for these vocabulary words. Your sentences should go with the first sentences.

1. blur <u>I felt myself getting very dizzy.</u>

   *Everything I looked at seemed to blur.*

2. momentarily <u>I worked for a very long time without stopping.</u>

   _____

3. glared <u>My teacher did not like how I was acting.</u>

   _____

# Writing: Punctuation

Use with student text page 82.

## Sentence Punctuation

Sentences end with one of three punctuation marks: a period, a question mark, or an exclamation mark.

A **period** ends a statement or a command.

The oak tree has green leaves**.**

Come downstairs**.**

A **question mark** ends a sentence that asks a question.

Would you like to go to computer camp**?**

An **exclamation point** ends a sentence that expresses strong emotion.

I hate computer camp**!**

➤ Edit these sentences. Rewrite each sentence adding the missing punctuation mark at the end of each sentence.

1. I could see the backyard from my bedroom window

   *I could see the backyard from my bedroom window.*

2. Why can't I think of an idea for my novel

   _____

3. I could hear my mother and father talking

   _____

4. She asked him if he thought I would be surprised

   _____

5. What surprise is she talking about

   _____

6. Don't tell me they are planning to send me to camp

   _____

7. How can I get out of it

   _____

8. This is going to ruin my summer

   _____

Name _____ Date _____

**Analyze Characters**

An author can use a character's actions to tell you what the character is like. Look at the chart below.

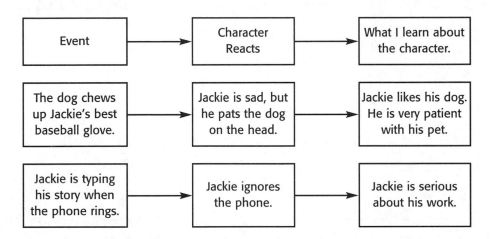

➤ Read the sentences. Then write what you learn about each character.

**1.** Jackie is typing his story when his father calls him to breakfast. Jackie yells back irritably.
**What I learn about Jackie:**

_____

_____

**2.** Jackie says he is getting too old for Saturday morning breakfasts. His father tells him to have a muffin.
**What I learn about Jackie's father:**

_____

_____

**3.** Jackie's father passes him a plate of muffins. He makes a disgusted face and ignores the muffins.
**What I learn about Jackie:**

_____

_____

**4.** Jackie's parents announce that they are sending him to camp. They are shocked and silent when he angrily leaves the room.
**What I learn about Jackie's parents:**

_____

_____

# Word Study

Use with student text page 84.

## Determine Word Meaning by Identifying Latin Roots

Many English words come from Latin. You can often figure out a word's meaning if you know the meaning of the Latin root.

The word *invisible* has the word part *vis. Vis* comes from a Latin word that means "see." The word *invisible* means "not able to be seen."

Several different words can have the same root. For example:

<u>vis</u>ion       (the ability to see)

<u>vis</u>it       (go to see someone or something)

<u>vis</u>ible       (able to be seen)

**A.** ➤ Look at the chart. Underline the root in each English word.

| Latin Root | Meaning | English Word |
|---|---|---|
| **1.** *aud* | hear | <u>aud</u>ible |
| **2.** *posit* | place or put | deposit |
| **3.** *cap* | take or seize | capture |
| **4.** *sat* | fill completely | satisfy |
| **5.** *trad* | hand over | tradition |

**B.** ➤ Write the English words from the chart next to their definitions.

**1.** passing of customs from one generation to another _____

**2.** meet or fill the needs of something completely _____

**3.** able to be heard _____

**4.** take and hold by force _____

**5.** put something in a safe place, such as in a bank _____

# Grammar Focus

*Use with student text page 85.*

## Use Progressive Tenses

**Progressive tenses** describe actions that are happening at a point in time. **Progressive tense verbs** always end with the letters *-ing*. For example, *walk**ing**.*

| Present and Past Progressive Tenses | | | |
|---|---|---|---|
| | **Subject** | **Auxiliary Verb** | **-Ing Verb** |
| **Present Progressive Tense** | I<br>You<br>He, She, It<br>We<br>They | am<br>are<br>is<br>are<br>are | going |
| **Past Progressive Tense** | I<br>You<br>He, She, It<br>We<br>They | was<br>were<br>was<br>were<br>were | going |

**A.** ➤ Complete each sentence with the correct auxiliary verb.

**Present Progressive**

1. Jackie _____ *is* _____ planning to skip breakfast.

2. Mom and Dad _____ waiting for Jackie.

3. They _____ hoping that he will like his surprise.

**Past Progressive**

1. Jackie _____ working on his novel late last night.

2. I _____ talking to him on the phone earlier this evening.

3. Mom and Dad _____ wondering what Jackie would say.

**B.** ➤ Edit these sentences. Rewrite each sentence using the correct auxiliary verb.

1. The wind were blowing while we were having a picnic.

_____

2. We is waiting for Jackie to finish his lunch.

_____

VISIONS C Activity Book • Copyright © Heinle

# Grammar Focus

Use with student text page 85.

## Use Progressive Tense Negatives, Contractions, and Questions

When adding *not* to a sentence, it becomes **negative.** A negative verb form shows an opposite action.

She is <u>not</u> going to the party.

They are <u>not</u> home.

You can also use a **contraction** for negative verb forms.

| Full Negative Verb | Negative Contraction |
|---|---|
| is not | isn't |
| are not | aren't |
| was not | wasn't |
| were not | weren't |

To form questions, put the auxiliary verb (*am, is, are, was, were*) in front of the subject.

Statement:    He <u>is</u> planning to go to camp.

Question:    <u>Is</u> he planning to go to camp?

➤ Follow the directions for rewriting each of the following sentences.

1. Rewrite these sentences as questions:
   **a.** He is playing for our team this summer.

   *Is he playing for our team this summer?*
   _____

   **b.** They were planning for him to begin next week.

   _____

2. Rewrite these sentences using a full negative verb:
   **a.** He is playing for our team this summer.

   _____

   **b.** They were planning for him to begin next week.

   _____

3. Rewrite each of these three sentences using a negative contraction:
   **a.** He is playing for our team this summer.

   _____

Student Handbook

   **b.** They were planning for him to begin next week.

   _____

Name _____   Date _____

# From Reading to Writing

*Use with student text page 85.*

## Edit Realistic Fiction

➤ Use the checklist to edit the realistic fiction you wrote in Chapter 1.

**Editing Checklist for Realistic Fiction**

Title of story: _____

**What I did:**

_____ **1.** I started the story at the point when Jackie left the kitchen.

_____ **2.** I used Mom and Dad as the characters.

_____ **3.** I wrote dialogue that helped develop characters.

_____ **4.** I used the past progressive tense correctly.

_____ **5.** I wrote a resolution to the conflict between Jackie and his parents.

_____ **6.** I indented all paragraphs.

## Across Content Areas

Use with student text page 85.

### Read a Chart

➤ Read this chart to learn more about the main nutrients the body uses.

| Main Nutrients That Provide Energy | | |
|---|---|---|
| Types of Nutrients | What It Is Used For | Food That Contains It |
| Protein | Protein is a nutrient in all living things. Protein helps the body grow and heal. | Foods that have a lot of protein are meat, fish, eggs, cheese, and milk. |
| Carbohydrate | Carbohydrates are a very important source of energy. | Macaroni, rice, corn, and potatoes have a lot of carbohydrates. Candy and soda also have a lot of carbohydrates, but too much of these foods is not good for you. |
| Fats | Fats have much more energy than proteins or carbohydrates. Fat can be used when the body does not receive food. | Fats are found in meat, butter, salad oils, fish, milk, eggs, and nuts. |

➤ Answer the questions. Use the chart.

1. What is this chart about?

   _____

2. Write the three headings of the chart.

   _____

3. What are the three main types of nutrients?

   _____

4. If you wanted to find foods that have a lot of carbohydrates, where would you look?

   _____

5. What information about nutrients is shown in the second column?

   _____

6. Write one food that has a lot of both protein and fat.

   _____

# Build Vocabulary

*Use with student text page 87.*

## Define Words and Read Dictionary Entries

**Understand Word Meanings**

A. ➤ Complete each sentence with the correct word found below.

**Word and Definition**

**dusk**  the period between sunset and night
**bridge**  part of a ship where the officers stand to give orders
**helm**  the wheel used to steer a ship
**swells**  long, unbroken waves on the ocean
**screeched**  made a loud, high sound
**fuel**  anything that is burned to give heat or energy
**label**  the marker on a product that lists its name and contents

**Sentences**

1. David could feel the ocean _____ gently lifting the boat.

2. Above the boat, a seagull _____.

3. David could barely see the ship in the _____.

4. He saw the captain standing on the _____.

5. David looked at the _____ on each can of food.

6. He needed more _____ for his stove.

7. David saw a man standing at the _____, steering a boat toward him.

**Locate Part of Speech of Words in a Dictionary**

Dictionaries show the part of speech of a word. Abbreviations (shortened spellings of words) are sometimes used to indicate the part of speech.

v. = verb      adj. = adjective      n. = noun      adv. = adverb

B. ➤ Look at this dictionary entry. Answer the question.

**dusk** /dʌsk/ *n.* the period late in the day between sunset and night just after the sun goes down: *It's hard to see at dusk, so I drive carefully.*

1. What part of speech is *dusk*?

_____

# Writing: Punctuation

*Use with student text page 98.*

## Punctuate Dialogue

**Dialogue** is the exact words that characters say. Dialogue is shown by placing quotation marks ("...") around the words that are spoken.

Quotation marks always go at the beginning and end of the spoken words.

Periods, commas, question marks, and exclamation marks usually go inside quotation marks.

David said, **"**Hey! Where are you going?**"**

**"**It's him! It's the boy everyone is looking for,**"** said the captain.

**A.** ➤ Rewrite the sentences by placing quotation marks to show dialogue.

1. Where am I? he said to the captain.

   *"Where am I?" he said to the captain.*

2. You are a long way from home, he said.

   _____

3. What's your name? asked the captain.

   _____

4. My name is David, he said.

   _____

5. David asked, Are they looking for me?

   _____

6. You bet they are! answered the captain.

   _____

7. Why are you here? asked David.

   _____

8. The captain said, We are a whale research ship.

   _____

# Elements of Literature

*Use with student text page 99.*

## Identify Conflict

**External conflicts** are problems a character has with things in nature or other people. **Internal conflicts** are problems within a character. For example, a character has an internal conflict when trying to overcome fear.

**A.** ➤ Write whether the conflict in each sentence is internal or external.

1. Daniel tried to hold on to his papers. The wind kept blowing them away.

   _____*external*_____

2. Maria wanted to go to the party, but she was too shy. _____*internal*_____

3. Pablo tried to get his dog to stop barking. _____

4. Viva wants to be a singer, but she is afraid to perform on stage. _____

5. Peter wants to join the soccer team, but he is worried that he is not very good.

   _____

6. Elizabeth really wanted to go to the mall, but her mother would not let her.

   _____

**B.** ➤ Write your own sentences that describe a conflict. Write whether the conflict is internal or external.

|  | Conflict | Internal or External |
|---|---|---|
| 1. | _____ | _____ |
| 2. | _____ | _____ |
| 3. | _____ | _____ |

VISIONS C Activity Book • Copyright © Heinle

**VISIONS Unit 2 • Chapter 2** The Voyage of the *Frog*

# Word Study

*Use with student text page 100.*

## Understand the Suffix *-ly*

A **suffix** is a group of letters added to the end of a word. A suffix can change the meaning of the word.

When the suffix *-ly* is added to an adjective, the new word is usually an **adverb.** Adverbs describe verbs. They help readers form pictures of the actions in their minds.

**A.** ➤ Fill in the chart. Form adverbs by adding *-ly* to each adjective.

| Adjective | Add *-ly* | New Word (Adverb) | Meaning |
|---|---|---|---|
| **1.** slow | + *-ly* | | in a slow way |
| **2.** quiet | + *-ly* | | in a quiet way |
| **3.** safe | + *-ly* | | in a safe way |
| **4.** rough | + *-ly* | | in a rough way |

**B.** ➤ Complete the sentences. Use the adverbs in the chart.

**1.** It was a long day. Finally, the sun sank _____ out of sight.

**2.** The large waves beat _____ against the side of the boat.

**3.** David's parents wanted him to return _____.

**4.** There was no noise. He only heard the wind whispering _____ in the sails.

**C.** ➤ Write four sentences of your own with the adverbs in the chart.

**1.** _____

**2.** _____

**3.** _____

**4.** _____

# Grammar Focus

*Use with student text page 100.*

## Use the Future Tense

You can use the word *will* to tell about future actions. *Will* is an auxiliary verb that is used with the simple form of a verb to make a **future tense verb.**

|  | **Affirmative Statement** | **Negative Statement** |
|---|---|---|
| Full Form | I **will arrive** tomorrow. | I **will not arrive** tomorrow. |
| Contracted Form | **I'll arrive** tomorrow | I **won't arrive** tomorrow. |

**A.** ➤ Complete the sentences. Follow the directions in parentheses for writing the future tense.

1. David _____*will not*_____ leave the boat. (full negative)

2. I _____ call his parents. (contracted affirmative)

3. They _____ be happy to hear he is safe. (full affirmative)

4. They _____ be happy to hear he is not coming home. (contracted negative)

5. David _____ sail the boat home by himself. (full affirmative)

**B.** ➤ Edit the paragraph. Find and correct the errors in the verbs.

Tomorrow, David will sail at sunrise. His friends and I have a party for him tonight. We not will see him for a long time. I get up early to tell him goodbye. He will be away for over two months. We miss him very much.

_____

_____

_____

_____

_____

_____

_____

_____

_____

_____

_____

**VISIONS Unit 2 • Chapter 2** The Voyage of the Frog

# Grammar Focus

*Use with student text page 100.*

## Use Prepositional Phrases of Time

A **prepositional phrase** is a group of words that begins with a preposition such as *in, at,* or *on.* Prepositional phrases that refer to a certain time are often used with the future tense.

> In the morning, I will finish my homework.

> The party will begin at seven o'clock.

> On Tuesday afternoon, the ship will leave port.

The prepositional phrases "in the morning," "at seven o'clock," and "on Tuesday afternoon" refer to the time of each future action.

**A.** ➤ Circle the future tense verbs and underline the prepositional phrases of time in each sentence.

1. In July, David will begin his trip.

2. His parents will not leave for home on Saturday.

3. At midnight, the captain will sail from here.

4. He will reach the island in the afternoon.

**B.** ➤ Think about your future for the next five years. Write your goals using the future tense. Use prepositional phrases of time to elaborate your written ideas.

1. _____

   _____

2. _____

   _____

3. _____

   _____

4. _____

   _____

Student
Handbook

# From Reading to Writing

Use with student text page 101.

## Edit a Story

➤ Use the checklist to edit the adventure story you wrote in Chapter 2.

**Editing Checklist for an Adventure Story**

Title of adventure story: _____

**What I did:**

_____ **1.** I described the characters.

_____ **2.** I described the problem, the cause of the problem, and how the characters solve the problem.

_____ **3.** I wrote a beginning, a middle, and an end.

_____ **4.** I used adverbs to make my writing more clear.

VISIONS **Unit 2 • Chapter 2** The Voyage of the Frog

## Across Content Areas

*Use with student text page 101.*

### Read a Map

The map below shows places from the story "The Voyage of the *Frog*." It shows the path that David traveled.

The map also shows a compass rose. A **compass rose** is a picture of a compass that shows directions. On a map, the compass always points to the north.

**A.** ➤ Answer the questions. Use the map.

1. What direction did David's boat travel?

   *south*

2. Is the city of Ventura north or south of where David's boat was found?

   *north*

3. Which city is farther north, San Diego or Los Angeles?

   _____

4. In what state is the city of San Diego?

   _____

5. What state is east of California?

   _____

6. In what ocean was David sailing?

   _____

# Build Vocabulary

Use with student text page 103.

## Use Words with Multiple Meanings

Words can have more than one meaning. Look at the words and meanings in the chart.

| Words With More Than One Meaning | | |
|---|---|---|
| **Words** | **Meaning 1** | **Meaning 2** |
| **1.** patterns | ways that do not change | the arrangement of design |
| **2.** tap | a device that turns the flow of liquid on and off | hit lightly |
| **3.** treated | exposed to a process | acted toward someone or something in a certain way |
| **4.** factor | a fact to be considered | a number that is multiplied to make another number |
| **5.** significant | large or meaningful | having a hidden meaning |
| **6.** familiarity | experience with or knowledge of | a close friendship |
| **7.** distant | acting in a way that is unconcerned or detached | far away or separated from a specific time or place |

**A.** ➤ Answer the questions. Use the definitions in the chart.

1. Which word can be used to talk about habits or designs? _____

2. Which word can be used to talk about friendship or knowledge? _____

**B.** ➤ Write whether the underlined word refers to Meaning 1 or Meaning 2.

1. I cannot decide which of these two wallpaper <u>patterns</u> to choose. _____*Meaning 2*_____

2. They <u>treated</u> the water with chemicals to make it safe to drink. _____

3. Now it is safe to drink water from the <u>tap</u>. _____

4. She gave a <u>significant</u> wave to secretly tell she was leaving. _____

5. Safety is the most important <u>factor</u> when traveling. _____

6. My father's <u>familiarity</u> with these roads makes us feel safe. _____

7. My <u>distant</u> relatives moved to the United States from England. _____

# Writing: Spelling and Punctuation

*Use with student text page 112.*

## Spell and Punctuate Contractions

**Contractions** make words shorter. They are formed by joining two words together. Letters are dropped and replaced by an apostrophe (').  Use contractions in speech and in informal writing.

| Full Form | Contraction | Letters Dropped |
|---|---|---|
| is not | isn't | o |
| are not | aren't | o |
| did not | didn't | o |
| I will | I'll | w, i |
| he has | he's | h, a |
| they have | they've | h, a |

| Full Form | Contraction | Letters Dropped |
|---|---|---|
| I am | I'm | a |
| they are | they're | a |
| we are | we're | a |
| there is | there's | i |
| it is | it's | i |

**A.** ➤ Rewrite the sentences by replacing the underlined words with contractions.

1. <u>I am</u> very afraid of poisonous snakes.

   *I'm very afraid of poisonous snakes.*

2. The risk of being bitten by a snake <u>is not</u> very big.

   _____

3. There <u>are not</u> many poisonous snakes in this area.

   _____

4. <u>They are</u> found mostly in the desert.

   _____

5. I know <u>it is</u> safe, but flying in an airplane still scares me.

   _____

**B.** ➤ Edit the following paragraph. Correct spelling and punctuation errors in the contractions.

My parents want me to give up skateboarding. They'ev read that skateboarding is dangerous. I"m really upset about it. My friends and I are planning to go skateboarding this weekend. Ther'es a new place we've heard about where everyone goes to skateboard. We're planning to ask Felicia and Ena to go. They'ar sisters, and they've just moved here. I guess I'l have to make some other plans. My parents arent going to change their minds.

# Elements of Literature

*Use with student text page 113.*

## Use Transition Words to Show Chronological Order

**Transition words** are used to connect ideas. They help organize sentences and paragraphs.

Transition words can be used to show **chronological order** (the order in which events occur). Transition words such as *first, second, next,* and *then* connect one event to the next.

| | |
|---|---|
| first | before |
| second | after |
| third | soon |
| next | later |
| then | recently |
| finally | |

**A.** ➤ Underline the transition words that show chronological order.

One of my favorite things to do is to go on trips to visit my grandmother. Before we begin, my father takes the car to the mechanic to make sure it is working right. Then, on the day of the trip, we wake up early in the morning. First we have a big breakfast. Next, we put all our suitcases and packages into the trunk of the car. Then we are ready to go. We drive all day long. Finally, we arrive at grandmother's house. She has a big dinner waiting for us. After eating, we all sit around the table and tell stories. That is the best part of the day.

**B.** ➤ Fill in each blank in the paragraph. Use the transition word that fits best.

I follow the same steps when I work in the garden. _____ I put on my old clothes. _____ I go to the garage where the tools are kept. _____ I pull up all the weeds in the garden. _____ I water all the plants. _____ I put all my tools back in the garage. _____ I sit next to the garden and drink a big glass of iced tea.

Name _____  Date _____

# Word Study

*Use with student text page 114.*

### Define Words with the Prefixes *Over-* and *Under-*

A **prefix** is a group of letters added to the beginning of a word. Knowing the meaning of a prefix can help you understand the meaning of a word.

The prefix *over-* means "too much." The prefix *under-* means "not enough." Look at the examples below:

**over**worked = worked too much

**under**worked = not worked enough

➤ Follow the directions to add a prefix to each root word. Then write a sentence using the new word.

1. **cooked** (add *over-*)

    *I overcooked the pizza so it is a little burned.*

2. **crowded** (add *over-*)

    _____

3. **develop** (add *under-*)

    _____

4. **protect** (add *over-*)

    _____

5. **estimate** (add *under-*)

    _____

6. **priced** (add *over-*)

    _____

7. **reacted** (add *over-*)

    _____

8. **dressed** (add *over-*)

    _____

VISIONS  Unit 2 • Chapter 3  To Risk or Not to Risk

VISIONS C  Activity Book • Copyright © Heinle

**60**

# Grammar Focus

Use with student text page 114.

## Use the Present Tense and Subject-Verb Agreement

The **present tense** describes actions that are generally true or that happen regularly.

We <u>walk</u> to school.

He <u>walks</u> to school.

Notice that in the second sentence an *s* was added to the verb *walk*. When the subject of a sentence is *he, she,* or *it,* you must add an *s* to present tense verbs.

| The Simple Present—Regular Verbs | | |
|---|---|---|
| I, you, we, they | wear<br>buy<br>want | shoes |
| he, she, it | wears<br>buys<br>wants | |

**A.** ➤ Write the correct form of the verb *work* next to the subject.

1. I _____*work*_____.

2. He _____*works*_____.

3. We _____.

4. You _____.

5. She _____.

6. It _____.

**B.** ➤ Rewrite the sentences below using the proper form of the verb found in parentheses. The first one has been done for you.

1. When it is nice outside, she (walk/walks) to school.

   *When it is nice outside, she walks to school.*

2. They (run/runs) when they want to exercise.

   _____

3. You (play/plays) soccer on the weekend.

   _____

4. When the weather is bad, he (read/reads) a book.

   _____

5. We (play/plays) tennis in the spring and summer.

   _____

6. She (want/wants) to become a doctor when she gets older.

   _____

# Grammar Focus

*Use with student text page 114.*

## Use the Present Tense and Subject-Verb Agreement in Sentences

You must also add an *-s* to the verb if the subject is a noun that can be replaced with *he, she,* or *it*. Look at these examples.

Joseph (He) exercise**S** every day.

Maria (She) write**S** a letter to her grandmother every week.

The music (It) sound**S** too loud.

**A.** ➤ Underline the correct verb in each sentence. The first one has been done for you.

1. The rattle (make/<u>makes</u>) a soft sound.

2. It (warn/warns) people to stay away from the snake.

3. Spiders (scare/scares) people.

4. People (avoid/avoids) them if possible.

5. Maria (turn/turns) on the light as soon as it gets dark outside.

6. She always (play/plays) the radio when she goes to bed.

7. Johnny (like/likes) to explore caves.

8. He (think/thinks) exploring is a challenge.

**B.** ➤ Write a sentence on each of the lines below using the form of the verb in parentheses. The first one has been done for you.

1. (walks) *He walks the dog every day.* _____

2. (drive) _____

3. (swims) _____

4. (wait) _____

5. (sleeps) _____

6. (rides) _____

7. (explore) _____

8. (completes) _____

Student
Handbook

# From Reading to Writing

*Use with student text page 115.*

## Write an Introduction

A good introduction will get your readers' attention. The chart shows some ways to write introductions.

| Type of Introduction | Example |
|---|---|
| Begin with an interesting fact. | When my grandmother was young, she was a famous chef at a restaurant in Paris. She made all of the desserts. |
| Use a vivid description. | Grandmother's kitchen always had a warm, sweet smell, like she had just taken cookies out of the oven. The aroma of sugar and spices always hung in the air. |
| Ask a question. | Do you remember the smell of your grandmother's kitchen when she was baking cookies? |
| Use dialogue. | "Guess where we are going today!" my father said in an excited voice. |

**A.** ➤ Write an introduction of one or two sentences for an informational text. Use one of the types of introductions shown in the chart.

_____

_____

_____

_____

_____

_____

## Across Content Areas

Use with student text page 115.

### Understand a Table of Contents

A **table of contents** is usually at the front of a textbook. It shows how the book is organized. The table of contents lists the name of each chapter. It also lists the page on which each chapter begins.

➤ Answer the questions. Use the table of contents.

1. What question does the first chapter answer?

   _____

2. On what page does chapter two begin?

   _____

3. What is the title of chapter three?

   _____

4. In what chapter would you look to learn how your family affects your behavior?

   _____

5. What chapter tells about how habits are formed?

   _____

# Build Vocabulary

Use with student text page 117.

## Define Words

**A.** ➤ Use the context to match the underlined word in each sentence to its definition.

**Word in a Sentence**

1. ___*f*___ Karana scooped out the dirt with her hands.

2. _____ She gathered bones to build a fence.

3. _____ She covered the embers so she could build another fire later.

4. _____ She collected reeds where they grew by the water.

5. _____ The roof of her house shed rain water and did not leak.

6. _____ She used lumps of clay by shaping them into pots.

7. _____ She bound the poles together so the house would be strong.

**Definition**

a. collected, brought in

b. long stems of certain plants

c. very hot pieces of wood remaining after a fire

d. make run off without going through

e. small, solid pieces of something that have no particular shape

f. dug out with the hands or a tool

g. fastened or tied

**B.** ➤ Write the letter of the phrase that completes each sentence. The first one has been done for you.

1. She scooped the potatoes ___*c*___

2. She gathered her books into _____

3. She added wood to _____

4. The green reeds look like _____

5. She wears her hat in the rain _____

6. He shaped the lumps of _____

7. Susan bound the pages of _____

a. dough into loaves of bread.

b. the embers in the fireplace.

c. out of the pot with a spoon.

d. the report together with glue.

e. because it sheds water.

f. a large backpack.

g. tall blades of grass.

# Writing: Punctuation

Use with student text page 126.

## Use Commas After Introductory Phrases

An **introductory phrase** is a group of words that begins a sentence. It appears before the subject of the sentence.

A comma (**,**) is used to separate the introductory phrase from the main part of the sentence. The main part of the sentence often begins with the subject.

subj<br>
|For a place to go in and out,||I dug a hole under the fence.|<br>
introductory phrase         main part of sentence

Sometimes the main part of the sentence begins with a **modifier,** which is a word that modifies, or describes, the subject.

modifier subject<br>
|Many years before,||two whales had washed up on shore.|<br>
introductory phrase         main part of sentence

**A.** ➤ Rewrite the sentences by adding the missing comma to separate the introductory phrase from the main part of the sentence.

1. Early in the morning she went to search for shellfish.
   *Early in the morning, she went to search for shellfish.*

2. Using her new basket she collected wood to build a fire.
   _____

3. Pulling the bones out one by one Karana placed them in a pile.
   _____

4. Later in the afternoon she walked down to the water.
   _____

5. With its thick, sturdy leaves the plant made a good covering for the roof.
   _____

6. In the floor of her house she dug a hole for a fire.
   _____

**B.** ➤ Edit the paragraph. Add commas after introductory phrases.

Left alone on the island Karana worked hard to survive. First of all she had to find shelter. After building a fence she began to build a house. Every night before bed she covered the hot embers of her fire. In the morning she used the embers to start a new fire.

# Elements of Literature

Use with student text page 127.

## Compare and Contrast Themes and Ideas Across Texts

"Island of the Blue Dolphins" and "The Voyage of the *Frog*" share the theme of survival, but there are other themes that occur in only one of the stories.

**A.** ➤ Read the themes in the chart. Which themes go with the characters?

| Themes | Karana | David |
|---|---|---|
| Survival | ✓ | ✓ |
| Making a home | | |
| Loyalty (being faithful to people and things that you care about) | | |

**B.** ➤ Read these statements. Check the character that they go with (David, Karana, or both). Then check the theme.

| | Characters | | Themes | | |
|---|---|---|---|---|---|
| Statements | Karana | David | Making a home | Loyalty | Survival |
| 1. The character is alone in a dangerous situation. | | | | | |
| 2. The character refuses to leave a boat behind. | | | | | |
| 3. The character builds shelves. | | | | | |

**C.** ➤ Complete this paragraph. Use the information from the chart in Activity B.

"Island of the Blue Dolphins" and "The Voyage of the *Frog*" share the general

theme of _____. In both stories, the characters _____

_____ .The stories have other themes that are not the same. Karana, for

example, has been left alone on the island. Therefore, she must _____.

For example, she _____ and does other things to make herself

comfortable. In David's situation, at one point he could be saved by a ship, but

he does not take this opportunity because he _____. This

_____ to the boat is important in the story. In these stories, we see

how David and Karana learn to survive. We also see other themes that come from the

characters' specific situations.

# Word Study

Use with student text page 128.

## Spell Frequently Misspelled Words

Some words sound alike but have different spellings and meanings. Look at the following examples of *there, their,* and *they're.*

| Word | Meaning | Example |
|---|---|---|
| There | "in that place" *or* may be used to begin sentences to show that something exists | She lives *there*. *There* are birds in the trees. |
| Their | "belonging to them" possessive form of *they* | *Their* house had a roof made of leaves. |
| They're | a contraction of "they are" | *They're* working hard to survive. |

**A.** ➤ Underline the correct form of *there, their,* or *they're* in each sentence.

1. Karana keeps her food over (there/their/they're).

2. (There/Their/They're) are wild dogs on the island.

3. (There/Their/They're) always trying to steal food from Karana.

4. (There/Their/They're) leader is very dangerous.

5. Karana keeps the embers (there/their/they're) in the fireplace.

6. (There/Their/They're) hard to keep burning until morning.

7. Karana placed the baskets in (there/their/they're) place on the rock shelf.

8. The people did not leave many of (there/their/they're) things on the island.

**B.** ➤ Follow the instructions to write each sentence.

1. Write a sentence using *they're.*

_____

2. Write a sentence using *their.*

_____

3. Write a sentence using *there.*

_____

Name _____ Date _____

# Grammar Focus

*Use with student text page 128.*

## Identify the Past and the Past Perfect Tense

The **past tense** describes an action that happened at a specific time in the past. Regular past tense verbs have *-d* or *-ed* at the end.

Karana scoop<u>ed</u> out a hole for the fireplace.

Karana ti<u>ed</u> the poles together to make a house.

The **past perfect tense** describes an action that happened in the past *before* another action that happened in the past. Past perfect tense verbs use the auxiliary verb *had* plus the past participle of the verb. Past participles of regular verbs have *-d* or *-ed* at the end.

```
              past perfect tense                                 past tense
Karana had finished building her fence before the dogs arrived.
              happened first                                     happened after
```

**A.** ➤ Write the past tense and the past perfect tense of the verbs.

| Verb | Past Tense | Past Perfect Tense |
|---|---|---|
| 1. wash | *washed* | *had washed* |
| 2. store | | |
| 3. gather | | |
| 4. quarrel | | |
| 5. gaze | | |
| 6. deepen | | |
| 7. save | | |
| 8. cover | | |

**B.** ➤ Complete these sentences with the past tense or the past perfect tense of the verb in parentheses.

1. Karana _had covered_ (cover) her shelter with leaves before it _____ (rain).

2. We _____ (need) a new dictionary last week. It was lucky that we _____ (save) some money to buy it with.

3. The farmers _____ (gather) their crops before it got dark.

4. Juanita _____ (cook) lunch before we said that we _____ (want) pizza.

VISIONS Unit 2 • Chapter 4 Island of the Blue Dolphins

VISIONS C Activity Book • Copyright © Heinle

**69**

Name _____   Date _____

# Grammar Focus

*Use with student text page 128.*

## Use Past and Past Perfect Tense Questions, Negatives, and Contractions

You can add *did not* to a past tense verb form to make it negative. In a past tense negative use the simple form of the verb, not the past form.

The food **did not** taste very good.      She **did not** cook the food very long.

To make a negative past perfect tense, the word *not* is added between *had* and the past participle verb.

The food **had not** tasted very good until she added salt.

She **had not** cooked the food before today.

You can write negative past and past perfect tense verb forms as contractions.

| Full Negative Verb Form | Negative Contraction |
|---|---|
| did not | didn't |
| had not | hadn't |

When past and past perfect tense verbs are used in questions, the auxiliary verb *did* or *had* goes before the subject of the sentence.

Did Karana gather enough shellfish?      Had Karana gathered enough shellfish?

➤ Fill in the blanks using the verbs and verb tenses shown.

1. (gather/past perfect negative, full form) Karana _____ the reeds before the rains came.

2. (gaze/past tense question) Why _____ she _____ at the ocean?

3. (store/past perfect tense question) What _____ Karana _____ in the shelter?

4. (cover/past tense negative contraction) She _____ the shelter with seaweed.

5. (wash/past perfect tense negative contraction) She _____ the dishes when she went to bed.

Student Handbook

VISIONS C   Activity Book • Copyright © Heinle

# From Reading to Writing

Use with student text page 129.

## Edit Instructions

➤ Use the checklist to edit the instructions you wrote in Chapter 4.

**Editing Checklist for Instructions**

Title of instructions: _____

**What I did:**

_____ 1. I thought about the activity before I began writing.

_____ 2. I asked myself what steps must be taken to complete
the activity I wrote instructions for.

_____ 3. I listed the steps in chronological order.

_____ 4. I used the guide given in my textbook.

_____ 5. Each step I wrote tells the reader what to do.

_____ 6. I reread my instructions and corrected any errors that
I found.

Name _____   Date _____

# Across Content Areas

*Use with student text page 129.*

**Analyze Illustrations**

   **Illustrations** can often be used to communicate information. Analyze this illustration to learn more about Karana and the problems she faced.

➤ Answer the questions. Use the illustration.

1. What is the main thing you see in this picture?
   _____

2. What is the girl carrying?
   _____

3. Do you see any houses or any other people?
   _____

4. What animals and plants do you see in the picture?
   _____

5. What other things do you see in the picture?
   _____

6. Do you think it will be hard for this girl to survive alone on the island? Why?
   _____

# Build Vocabulary

*Use with student text page 131.*

## Use a Glossary and Categorize Words

A **glossary** is a list of words and definitions that often appears at the end of a textbook. Words in a glossary are usually listed in alphabetical order. Read these glossary definitions:

**catastrophe**  a great act of destruction or loss
**century**  one hundred years
**comets**  objects in outer space that move around the sun;
    they have long tails of burning material and sometimes
    can be seen from Earth
**engaged**  to be involved; participate
**glamorous**  seen as interesting or exciting
**predict**  say what you think will happen in the future
**resources**  things that are useful to people
**theories**  ideas about why something happens

**A.** ➤ Complete the sentences. Use the words from the glossary above.

1. Some people like to watch for _____ in the night sky.

2. She became _____ in saving animals in danger of extinction.

3. During the past _____, many species of animals have become extinct.

4. Scientists try to _____ which animals will be in the greatest danger.

5. There are several _____ that explain why animals become extinct.

6. Some scientists believe a comet crashed into Earth and caused a _____.

7. When our natural _____ are used up, many animals may become extinct.

8. People know about the more _____ species in danger of extinction.

## Categorize Words

A category is a group or type of something. For example, *clothing* can be a category for the words *hat, shoes, shirt, pants*.

**B.** ➤ Write a category for each list of words. Use words from the glossary.

_____     _____     _____

earthquakes          water          opinions
floods               trees          arguments
tornadoes            gold           speculations

Name _____  Date _____

# Writing: Capitalization

Use with student text page 140.

## Capitalize Proper Nouns

**Proper nouns** name specific people, places, and things. Proper nouns are always capitalized (begin with a big letter).

| | | | |
|---|---|---|---|
| **Nouns and Proper Nouns** | | | |
| **Nouns** | **Proper Nouns Referring to People** | **Proper Nouns Referring to Places** | **Proper Nouns Referring to Things** |
| woman | Elizabeth | Chicago | Statue of Liberty |
| man | Richard | United States | the Constitution |
| men and women | Native Americans | the Great Plains | the Great Depression |

**A.** ➤ Edit these sentences. Rewrite each sentence correcting capitalization errors.

1. During summer vacation, my Family is going to visit the grand canyon.
   *During summer vacation, my family is going to visit the Grand Canyon.*

2. The Boy told me his name was robert munoz.

3. In school today, We learned about the declaration of independence.

4. When we went to chicago, we saw the sears tower and lake michigan.

5. After school, Ben and his Sister went to the Family Reunion.

6. José's Grandparents are coming to visit from mexico.

7. Mrs. Ortiz, our Teacher, said the whole class did well on the test.

VISIONS Unit 2 • Chapter 5 The Next Great Dying

VISIONS C Activity Book • Copyright © Heinle

**74**

# Elements of Literature

*Use with student text page 141.*

## Analyze Deductive and Inductive Organization and Presentation

Authors use **deductive** organization and presentation to make a point. Then they give facts and examples to support their point.

Authors use **inductive** organization and presentation to give facts and examples first. They use the facts and examples to draw a conclusion.

**A.** ➤ Read the statements. Write whether deductive or inductive organization and presentation is used.

1. We are going to have a rainstorm soon. Black clouds are beginning to fill the sky. The wind is starting to blow hard. I just heard the weather reporter on the radio say that a storm is coming. _____

2. I am beginning to get hungry. The smell of food is coming from the cafeteria. It must be lunchtime. _____

3. My desk lamp is broken. It will not turn on. I made sure that it was plugged into the electrical outlet. I changed the light bulb, but it still will not turn on. _____

4. I found one of my good shoes under the bed. It was torn and ripped. There were big teeth marks on it. The dog chewed up my shoe. _____

**B.** ➤ Rewrite the statements using deductive and inductive organization and presentation.

My head aches.
My nose is stuffy.
I think I have a cold.
My throat hurts.

1. **Deductive Organization and Presentation**

   **Point or Statement:** _____

   **Supporting Fact 1:** _____

   **Supporting Fact 2:** _____

   **Supporting Fact 3:** _____

2. **Inductive Organization and Presentation**

   **Fact 1:** _____

   **Fact 2:** _____

   **Fact 3:** _____

   **Conclusion:** _____

# Word Study

Use with student text page 142.

## Identify the Suffix *-ion*

A **suffix** is a group of letters added to the end of a word. A suffix can change the meaning of the word.

When the suffix *-ion* is added to a verb, the new word is a **noun.** A noun names a person, place, or thing.

**A.** ➤ Fill in the chart. Form a noun by adding *-ion* to each verb.

| Verb | Add *-ion* | Noun |
|---|---|---|
| **1.** act | + *-ion* | |
| **2.** predict | + *-ion* | |
| **3.** connect | + *-ion* | |
| **4.** perfect | + *-ion* | |

**B.** ➤ Complete each sentence. Use the nouns you wrote in the chart.

1. Many scientists believe many species of animals will disappear. Many people agree with this _____.

2. Many animals will become extinct if people do not work to protect them. It is time to take _____.

3. Amal spent many hours trying to improve her report on dinosaurs. She tries for _____ in everything she does.

4. Scientists say they can relate the extinction of many species with what people do. Many people do not agree with this _____.

**C.** ➤ Write a sentence for each of the nouns you wrote in the chart.

1. _____

_____

2. _____

_____

3. _____

_____

4. _____

_____

## Grammar Focus

Use with student text page 142.

### Recognize Dependent Clauses

A **dependent clause** has a subject and a verb, but is not a complete sentence. It cannot stand alone.  It must be used with an independent clause. Many dependent clauses begin with the word *that*.

independent          dependent
clause              clause

Scientists say | that the animals are in trouble.

independent          dependent
clause              clause

Scientists say | that extinction is a serious problem.

The dependent clause tells us *what* the "scientists say."

**A.** ➤ Underline the dependent clauses in each sentence. The first one has been done for you.

1. Scientists hope <u>that they can slow down the rate of extinction.</u>

2. Scientists try to convince people that they should help solve the problem.

3. My friend believes that we should start a club to tell people about extinction.

4. She thinks that people should learn about the problem.

**B.** ➤ Rewrite the sentences above. Use the same independent clauses and add your own dependent clauses that start with *that*.

1. Scientists hope *that they can help some animals.* _____

2. _____

_____

3. _____

_____

4. _____

_____

# Grammar Focus

Use with student text page 142.

## Study Dependent Clauses and Complex Sentences

A **complex sentence** contains a main clause (or independent clause) and one or more dependent clauses.

independent    dependent
clause         clause

I agree that it is a problem.

independent       dependent          dependent
clause           clause             clause

Scientists say that we must change or the problem will become worse.

Notice that the length of a sentence does not determine whether a sentence is complex or simple. A complex sentence can be short or long.

**A.** ➤ Write *complex* next to the complex sentences. If the sentence is not a complex sentence, write *NOT*.

1. _____ He was sure that he saw a rare Bengal tiger in the jungle.

2. _____ Our class is ready to begin studying some extinct animals.

3. _____ We learned that many animals became extinct long ago.

4. _____ We know that many other animals are in danger of becoming extinct.

5. _____ A person from the zoo visited our class and told us that we can help save some animals from extinction.

**B.** ➤ Write a paragraph of four sentences about your favorite animal. Use at least one complex sentence in your paragraph.

_____

_____

_____

_____

Student
Handbook

Name _____ Date _____

# From Reading to Writing
## Edit an Informational Text

➤ Use the checklist to edit the informational text you wrote in Chapter 5.

**Editing Checklist for an Informational Text**

Title of informational text: _____

**What I did:**

_____ 1. I wrote an introduction, a body, and a conclusion.

_____ 2. I chose inductive or deductive organization and presentation for each paragraph.

_____ 3. I indented paragraphs.

_____ 4. I used some dependent clauses with *that* and punctuated them correctly.

_____ 5. I used present and future tenses and made sure the present tense verbs agreed with their subjects.

_____ 6. I used the model in my textbook to help me.

_____ 7. I reread my informational text and corrected any errors that I found.

Name _____   Date _____

## Across Content Areas

*Use with student text page 143.*

### Use Reference Sources

An **encyclopedia** is a book or set of books that gives information about different topics. Topics are listed in alphabetical order. Read this encyclopedia article to learn more about how dinosaurs died out. Notice how the author uses headings to tell you what a section is about.

**Why Did Dinosaurs Become Extinct?**

There are many different theories, or explanations, for why dinosaurs disappeared from the earth. However, most scientists believe in one of these theories:

**Climate Change** This theory states that the earth's climate began to change millions of years ago. Winters became colder. Summers became hotter. Dinosaurs could not survive in this new climate. They had no fur or feathers to protect them from cold. They probably had no way of keeping cool in the heat. As the climate changed to cold winters and hot summers, the dinosaurs began to die. Finally, they became extinct.

**Asteroid** Asteroids are icy rocks that fall to the earth from space. Scientists believe that a giant asteroid hit the earth about 65 million years ago. The asteroid hit the earth so hard that it caused a lot of heat. Fires spread all over the world. Clouds of smoke blocked the sunlight, causing the earth to grow cold. Plants stopped growing. Dinosaurs that depended on plants for food died. Dinosaurs that depended on other dinosaurs for food also died.

➤ Answer the questions. Use the encyclopedia article.

1. What is this article about? _____

2. What are the two headings in the article? _____

3. You want to learn about how the climate affected dinosaurs. Where in the article would you look? _____

4. Which of these two theories explain how dinosaurs died because of lack of food?

    _____

5. Write two sentences explaining the two main theories about why dinosaurs became extinct. _____

    _____

# Build Vocabulary

*Use with student text page 153.*

## Replace Words with Synonyms

**A.** ➤ Read the words and definitions in the box. Then circle the word in each group that does not belong.

**Word and Definition**

**blooming** flowering, blossoming
**echo** a repeated sound
**globe** a spherical representation of Earth or another planet
**humanity** kindness, compassion
**longing** wishing, desiring
**ornamented** decorated
**tranquil** peaceful, calm

1. wish, desire, longing, growing

2. globe, Earth, sword, planet

3. echo, repeat, repetition, sight

4. decorated, ornamented, quiet, beautiful

5. peaceful, quiet, noisy, tranquil

6. growing, flowering, blooming, dying

7. goodness, humanity, kindness, anger

**B.** ➤ Rewrite the paragraph by replacing each underlined word with a synonym from the list in Activity A.

### Journey to Utopia

You will not find Utopia on our <u>Earth</u>. You will not find it anywhere. It is a made-up place. It means "paradise on Earth." Do you have a <u>wish</u> to go somewhere wonderful? Then you can go to Utopia in your mind. It is a place where <u>goodness</u> rules. Maybe it is a <u>peaceful</u> garden, <u>flowering</u> all year. Or it could be a palace, richly <u>decorated</u> just for you. Or perhaps it is a beach where you hear the <u>repeated sound</u> of a seagull. Are any of these your idea of Utopia?

_____

_____

_____

# Writing: Spelling

Use with student text page 158.

## Learn Spelling Rules for Words Ending in Silent e

Many English words end with a **letter e** that is **silent,** such as *have* and *believe.*
Say these words aloud.

To add an ending that starts with a vowel, drop the silent *e*.

hav~~e~~ + -*ing* = hav**ing**

believ~~e~~ + -*ing* = believ**ing**

To add an ending that starts with a consonant, keep the silent *e*.

car**e** + -*ful* = car**eful**

lik**e** + -*ness* = lik**eness**

➤ Complete each sentence with the correct spelling of the word in parentheses.

1. Children around the world are (have + -*ing*) _____*having*_____ fun.

2. In northern countries, they are skiing on (peace + -*ful*) _____ hills.

3. The long days are (change + -*ing*) _____ to short and cold days.

4. Some warm places are (become + -*ing*) _____ rainy.

5. Other people are (make + -*ing*) _____ cold drinks out in the sun.

6. Plants are (live + -*ing*) _____ well.

7. At the South Pole, the sun is (shine + -*ing*) _____ 24 hours a day.

8. In warm weather, she likes (loose + -*ness*) _____ in her clothing.

VISIONS C  Activity Book • Copyright © Heinle

# Elements of Literature

*Use with student text page 159.*

## Identify Style

**Style** is a certain way of writing. It is made up of the author's choice of words and tone. It also is found in an author's sentence length, use of imagery, and dialogue.

Poets often use images based on the senses. **Sight, hearing, taste, touch,** and **smell** are the senses.

➤ Read the poem. Fill in the web with images from the poem. Find examples based on the five senses.

**Wild Horses**

Off to fields,
There you chase.
Up and down
The brush and **lace.**
Round and down
**Lily** white and
Prairie brown
Manes like
Butterflies swirling around.
Bearing your breath
**Gnashing** your teeth
Against the rush of leaves
Without windbreak.
Thunder hooves
And spirits high
Your run is like history
All in **rewind.**

**lace**  Queen Anne's
          lace; a white flower
**lily**  a green plant with
          white flowers
**gnashing**  grinding
          together
**rewind**  unravel; go
          backwards

Wild
Horses

# Word Study

Use with student text page 160.

## Make Nouns with the Suffix *-ity*

A **suffix** is a group of letters added to the end of a word. A suffix can change a word from one part of speech to another.

*Mature* is an **adjective.** It means "developed or grown."

The suffix *-ity* means "condition or state of."

If you add the suffix *-ity* to *mature,* the new word becomes a **noun.**

*Maturity* means the "condition or state of being developed or grown."

When you add the suffix *-ity* to a word that ends in *-e,* drop the *e.* Then add *-ity.*

**A.** ➤ Form a new word by adding *-ity* to each word. Then write the meaning.
   Use a dictionary to help you.

1. active          _____  _____

2. odd             _____  _____

3. scarce          _____  _____

4. sincere         _____  _____

5. human           _____  _____

**B.** ➤ Complete each sentence with a word ending in *-ity* from above.

1. Everyone liked her for her honesty and _____.

2. He did not like the science _____.

3. He won an award for his _____.

4. There is a _____ of food in the desert.

5. His strange hat is a(n) _____.

# Grammar Focus

*Use with student text page 160.*

## Use Apostrophes with Possessive Nouns

Possessive nouns show who "owns" something.

That's Ana's sweater.

| Noun | Ending | Examples |
|------|--------|----------|
| Singular Noun: girl, Irina | Add apostrophe + -s | The girl's name is Irina. What is in Irina's purse? |
| Singular Noun ending in -s: Texas | Add apostrophe only | Texas' people |
| Plural ending in -s girls | Add apostrophe only | The girls' names are Irina and Ivana. |

**A.** ➤ Rewrite the paragraph by writing the possessive form of each noun in parentheses.

Some people enjoy traveling for a living. (Keisha) _____*Keisha's*_____ job is to find (place) _____ to shoot movies. She also makes sure the (crew) _____ needs are taken care of. The (workers) _____ food and living arrangements must be adequate. (Suki) _____ job is to find crafts in Asia. Her (company) _____ stores sell interesting clothing and home items from all over the world. Suki loves looking in (Asia) _____ cities and villages. Brianna travels to her (bank) _____ offices in Europe and Africa. In her time off, she especially likes (Dakar) _____ music and (Rome) _____.

**B.** ➤ Write a sentence using the possessive form of each noun.

**1.** boys

_____

**2.** Karl

_____

**3.** tree

_____

**4.** buildings

_____

**5.** Carlos

_____

# Grammar Focus

Use with student text page 160.

## Use Irregular Plural Nouns

**Irregular plural nouns** are not formed by adding -*s*.
The plural form of *man* is *men*, not *mans*. Look at these irregular plural nouns:

| Singular | Plural |
|----------|--------|
| man | men |
| woman | women |
| child | children |
| foot | feet |

| Singular | Plural |
|----------|--------|
| mouse | mice |
| tooth | teeth |
| person | people |

To make the possessive form of irregular plural nouns, add apostrophe + *s*.
The children's lunch is ready.

➤ Edit these sentences. Rewrite each sentence with the correct plural form.

1. Many of the <u>womans</u> in my family are lawyers.
   *Many of the women in my family are lawyers.*

2. The <u>childs</u> in my class like their teacher.
   _____

3. My <u>foots</u> are aching after soccer practice.
   _____

4. Most of the <u>mans</u> in my family are over six feet tall.
   _____

5. My mother is afraid of <u>mouses</u>, but I think they are cute.
   _____

6. I brush my <u>teeths</u>.
   _____

7. Where did you put the <u>womens'</u> coat?
   _____

8. The <u>persons</u> work at the restaurant.
   _____

9. The dentist said that my <u>tooths</u> are ok.
   _____

# From Reading to Writing

*Use with student text page 161.*

## Edit a Poem

➤ Use the checklist to edit the poem you wrote in Chapter 1.

**Editing Checklist for a Poem Using Figurative Language**

Title of poem: _____

**What I did:**

_____ **1.** I wrote about a person I know.

_____ **2.** I separated the lines of my poem into stanzas.

_____ **3.** I used free verse. The ends of my lines do not rhyme.

_____ **4.** I described people, places, and things so readers can draw images.

_____ **5.** I uscd figurative language (especially metaphors) to describe the person.

_____ **6.** I repeated words to show strong feelings and important ideas.

_____ **7.** I used some possessive noun forms in my poem.

_____ **8.** I chose the form in which to present my poem for the effect I wanted.

Name _____  Date _____

## Across Content Areas
Use with student text page 161.

### Create a Data Chart

**Data** is facts or information. It is used to draw conclusions about a subject. Scientists use data in their research.

A **data chart** is a form to record data.

**A.** ➤ Find sources about birds that migrate, or travel. Look in science books and on the Internet. Ask people.

Take notes and record your data in the chart. Record your sources.

| Birds That Migrate Data Chart | | | | |
|---|---|---|---|---|
| Type of Bird | Migrates from | Migrates to | Distance Traveled (One Trip) | Sources |
|  |  |  |  |  |
|  |  |  |  |  |
|  |  |  |  |  |

**B.** ➤ Answer the questions. Use your chart.

1. Which birds fly the farthest distance?

_____

2. Which birds fly the shortest distance?

_____

3. What places do the birds migrate from?

_____

4. What places do the birds migrate to?

_____

VISIONS Unit 3 • Chapter 1 I Have No Address

VISIONS C Activity Book • Copyright © Heinle

# Build Vocabulary

*Use with student text page 163.*

### Define Words and Find Dictionary Head Words

**A.** ➤ Complete the sentences. Use the words in the box.

**Word and Definition**

| | |
|---|---|
| **rapped** struck | **declared** said |
| **rudely** without manners | **nervously** uneasily |
| **defensively** protectively | **gazing** staring |
| **abolished** stopped | **steadfastly** without changing |
| **shrugged** raised one's shoulders | |

1. I did not know the answer, so I _____ my shoulders.

2. Someone _____ loudly on the door while I was trying to study.

3. They are _____ at the stars.

4. I look _____ at my feet when I speak in public.

5. My dog is _____ loyal to me.

6. Vladimir was _____ the winner.

7. I extended my arms _____ to protect me from the fall.

8. I spoke _____ to my mother. I feel guilty.

9. At school, the teachers _____ chewing gum.

### List Head Words

Words are listed alphabetically in the dictionary. The words in boldface (dark) type are called **head words.**

Look for the simplest form of the word. This is often the root or base word.

For example, if you are looking for the word *started,* the head word will be *start.*

**B.** ➤ Fill in the chart. Write the head word in the dictionary for each word. The first one has been done for you.

| If you are looking up . . . | You will find it under . . . |
|---|---|
| **1.** rapped | rap |
| **2.** rudely | |
| **3.** gazing | |

# Writing: Capitalization

Use with student text page 174.

## Capitalize Proper Nouns

**Proper nouns** name specific people, places, and things. Proper nouns are always capitalized.

➤ Edit these sentences. Rewrite each sentence using correct capitalization. The first one has been done for you.

| People | Phon Thi Chi<br>Uncle Tan |
|--------|---------------------------|
| Places | Vietnam<br>United States |
| Things | Vietnam War<br>Communist Party |

1. Like several other Nations, france had colonies in asia.

   _Like several other nations, France had colonies in Asia._

2. During the early 20th century, vietnam was part of french Indochina.

   _____

3. After world war II, many people around the world fought for independence.

   _____

4. Many Vietnamese joined the fight against the french.

   _____

5. French indochina became four Countries: North Vietnam, South Vietnam, laos, and cambodia.

   _____

6. Communists were in charge of north vietnam.

   _____

7. They wanted to control south vietnam, too.

   _____

8. The united states sent soldiers to help the south vietnamese.

   _____

9. The Chinese sent soldiers to help the north Vietnamese.

   _____

10. When the fighting ended, vietnam became one country.

   _____

Name _____ Date _____

Use with student text page 175.

# Elements of Literature

**Recognize Mood**

**Mood** is a feeling that readers get from a text. Authors use words to create a mood. For example, authors can write to show anger, happiness, or humor.

**A.** ➤ Look at these webs. Each one has a mood in the center. Write four words for each web that help set the mood.

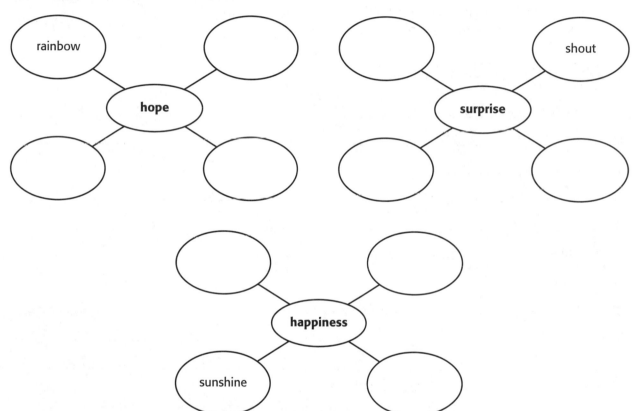

**B.** ➤ Choose one of the moods from the word webs above. Write a paragraph that expresses that mood. Use the words from the web.

_____

_____

_____

_____

_____

_____

_____

_____

# Word Study

Use with student text page 176.

## Analyze the Prefix -un

A **prefix** is a group of letters added to the beginning of a word.
A prefix can change the meaning of the word.

Use the meaning of the original word and the meaning of the prefix
to understand the meaning of the new word.

*Able* means having the power or skill to do something.

The prefix *-un* means "not."

*Unable* means "not able."

**A.** ➤ Write the meaning of each word.

1. unaware _____

2. unusual _____

3. uncomfortable _____

4. unbend _____

5. unimportant _____

6. unclear _____

7. uncertain _____

8. unbelievable _____

9. unlisted _____

10. unlock _____

**B.** ➤ Add the prefix -un to each word. Then write a sentence using the new word.

1. aware _____

_____

2. happy _____

_____

3. lock _____

_____

4. usual _____

_____

5. healthy _____

_____

# Grammar Focus

*Use with student text page 176.*

## Identify Subject and Object Pronouns

A **pronoun** is a word that takes the place of a noun. *She, he, her, him, me,* and *it* are all examples of pronouns. A pronoun can stand for the name of a person, place, or thing.

Uncle Tan wants to come along. <u>He</u> wants to come along.

Vietnam is in Asia. <u>It</u> is in Asia.

The store is closed. <u>It</u> is closed.

A **subject pronoun** is the subject of a sentence. When a pronoun is the subject, use one of the following words: *I, you, he, she, it, we,* and *they.* Use the word that fits the sentence.

**A. ➤** Write an answer to each question using the correct subject pronoun.

**1.** Did you enjoy reading about the Vietnamese family?

　　*Yes, I did enjoy reading about the Vietnamese family.*

**2.** What do you think of Phan Thi Chi?

　　_____

**3.** Why does Ah Soong live with the family?

　　_____

An **object pronoun** comes after a verb or prepositions like *from, far,* or *to.* *Me, you, him, her, it, us,* and *them* are object pronouns.

Give Uncle Tan the book. Give <u>him</u> the book.

**B. ➤** Rewrite the sentences by replacing the underlined object noun with the correct object pronoun.

**1.** All eyes were fixed on <u>Aunt Binh</u>.

　　*All eyes were fixed on her.*

**2.** The family members did not like <u>the young man</u>.

　　_____

**3.** They remembered <u>the Communist invasion</u>.

　　_____

**4.** During the Vietnam War, Americans learned a lot about <u>the Vietnamese people</u>.

　　_____

# Grammar Focus

*Use with student text page 176.*

## Use Subject and Object Pronouns

Use **subject pronouns** in sentences with **compound subjects** (more than one subject).

Correct: Toshio and I gave Diem a party.

Incorrect: Toshio and me gave Diem a party.

Always put the subject pronoun last.

Correct: Toshio and I went to the party.

Incorrect: I and Toshio went to the party.

Use **object pronouns** in sentences with **compound objects** (more than one object).

Gabriela spoke to Ana and Mario.

Correct: Gabriela spoke to her and him.

Incorrect: Gabriela spoke to she and he.

➤ Underline the correct pronoun. The first one has been done for you.

1. My grandma and ( I , me) were talking about the old days.

2. Sybil and (I, me) are looking for a movie theater.

3. I gave my father and (she, her) a school picture.

4. Phil and (me, I) decided not to go with Barbara and (she, her) to the game.

5. (Her, She) and (me, I) gave Fernando a tour of the museum.

6. The teacher gave Eliza and (I, me) a perfect score on our essays.

7. Leo mailed a letter to Francine and (he, him).

Student
Handbook

# From Reading to Writing

*Use with student text page 177.*

## Write from Another Point of View

**Point of view** is the perspective, or position, from which the story is told.

➤ This story is written from Emil's point of view. Rewrite it from Ricardo's point of view. He is telling the story. Use the pronouns *I, me,* and *my*.

**Emil's Story**

Ricardo went to the corner store with me. I wanted to buy a new book. I found a book. I went to the counter. I asked the lady a question. She was rude to me. Ricardo said she just looked tired. He thought she was nice but having a bad day. I was unhappy. I did not buy a book. Ricardo found three books that he liked. He has a positive attitude. I am lucky to have such a happy friend.

_____

_____

_____

_____

_____

_____

_____

_____

_____

_____

_____

_____

_____

_____

_____

_____

Name _____    Date _____

## Across Content Areas

Use with student text page 177.

### Give Map Directions

➤ Answer the questions. Use the map.

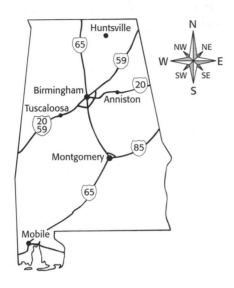

1. What direction would you travel to get from Anniston to Birmingham?

   _____

2. What road would you take from Birmingham to Montgomery?

   _____

   In what direction? _____

3. Mobile is what direction from Montgomery? _____

4. To go from Mobile to Huntsville, which two directions would you travel? First

   _____, then _____

5. Tuscaloosa is what direction from Huntsville? _____

# Build Vocabulary

**Define Words**

Use with student text page 179.

---

**Word and Definition**

**nook**  a small room
**croquet**  an outdoor game played by hitting a ball with a mallet
**mallets**  wooden-headed hammers
**phosphorescent**  a quality that makes something glow
**murmur**  a low, unclear sound
**speedometer**  an instrument that measures how fast something is going
**fender**  a part of a bike that protects the wheel
**oval**  shaped like an egg

---

➤ Complete the sentences. Use the words in the box.

1. I can see my watch in the dark because it is _____.

2. With the door closed, the noise down the hall was reduced to a _____.

3. _____ is a fun game to play in the yard during a barbecue.

4. The object of the game is to hit the ball with _____.

5. When I need a quiet place to read, I find a little _____ in the corner of my room.

6. An egg is not a circle; it is an _____.

7. To check the speed when I am driving, I look at the _____.

8. The _____ on my bike keeps water from spraying as I ride.

# Writing: Capitalization and Punctuation

*Use with student text page 188.*

## Capitalize and Punctuate Dialogue

**Quotation marks** (" ") are placed before and after the exact words that a character says. If the sentence continues after the quotation, use a comma after the spoken words.

**"**It is a beautiful day,**"** she exclaimed.

When the dialogue appears at the end of a sentence, the first letter of the dialogue should be capitalized.

As I left for school, my father said, "**G**ood luck on your test."

When there are quotations at the beginning and end of a sentence, commas should separate them from the rest of the sentence. The quotation at the end of the sentence should not be capitalized.

"Eddy**,**" said Uncle Freddy**,** "would you move it?"

➤ Edit these sentences. Rewrite each sentence correcting the capitalization and punctuation errors.

1. "Lets take a look at that bike." said Uncle Freddy.

   _____

   _____

2. "I'll bring my wrench set" Eddy answered.

   _____

   _____

3. "I don't think wrenches will fix what is wrong, Uncle Freddy said.

   _____

   _____

4. "What do you suggest then asked Eddy."

   _____

   _____

5. Just then they heard a voice call "Eddy and Freddy! Time for lunch."

   _____

   _____

Name _____  Date _____

# Elements of Literature

*Use with student text page 189.*

**Recognize Foreshadowing**

Authors often give clues about what will happen later in the story. This is called **foreshadowing.**

➤ Circle the event that could be foreshadowed in each sentence.

1. Storm clouds gathered, and the wind began to blow.
   a. It was a perfect day to go sailing.
   b. We brought the boat ashore as quickly as we could.

2. We tied up the boat and ran for shelter.
   a. Just then, the rain began pelting the roof.
   b. There was a huge feast waiting for us.

3. We thought we would have to wait a long time for the storm to end.
   a. James looked around the boathouse to see if there was anything to eat.
   b. We ran for the nearest bus.

4. James found nothing but a box of crackers.
   a. "I'll go to the grocery store and get us lunch," said Trish.
   b. "This is all we'll have to eat until the storm lets up," said Trish.

5. After we ate, there was nothing much to do.
   a. We got the boat and took it out again.
   b. We decided to sleep until the rain stopped.

VISIONS C Activity Book • Copyright © Heinle

VISIONS Unit 3 • Chapter 3 The Time Bike

# Word Study

Use with student text page 190.

## Analyze the Prefix bi-

A **prefix** is a group of letters added to the beginning of a word. A prefix can change the meaning of the word.

The prefix *bi-* means "two." When *bi-* is added to the word *cycle*, which means "wheel," the new word means "a machine with two wheels."

**A.** ➤ Answer the questions. Use the words and their meanings to help you.

**1. biannual** every two years. How many months is that?

_____

**2. bicultural** two distinct cultures. Can you name something that is bicultural?

_____

**3. bicolor** of two colors. Name something that is bicolor.

_____

**4. bimonthly** every two months. About how many days is that?

_____

**5. bipedal** having two feet. Name something that is bipedal.

_____

**B.** ➤ Write sentences using the words with the prefix *bi-*.

**1.** biannual

_____

**2.** bicultural

_____

**3.** bicolor

_____

**4.** bimonthly

_____

**5.** bipedal

_____

# Grammar Focus

Use with student text page 190.

## Write Using Contractions

An **auxiliary verb** is a verb that combines with another verb. Some auxiliary verbs can be contracted (shortened). The letters that are taken out are replaced by an apostrophe ('). Use contractions in speech and in informal writing.

| Auxiliary Verb | Contracted Form | Example |
|---|---|---|
| am | 'm | I'm a soccer player. |
| is | 's | He's a gymnast. |
| are | 're | We're friends. |
| have | 've | I've been to Paris. |
| has | 's | She's been to Paris. |
| had | 'd | I'd been gone. |
| will | 'll | We'll be gone. |
| would | 'd | I thought I'd be gone. |

➤ Complete each sentence with the contraction of the two words in parentheses.

1. (We are) _____ expecting the delivery of a special bicycle.

2. (It is) _____ a special delivery.

3. (We have) _____ ordered a magical bicycle.

4. (I will) _____ be able to go back in time.

5. (I have) _____ always wanted to visit ancient Rome.

6. (We will) _____ finally get to meet Julius Caesar.

7. Perhaps (he will) _____ want to talk to me.

8. (I had) _____ better learn some Latin first.

9. (I would) _____ ask you to come along, but there is only room for one.

Name _____     Date _____

# Grammar Focus

*Use with student text page 190.*

## Write Using Negative Contractions

The contracted form of *not (n't)* can be added to some auxiliary verbs to make them **negative.**

She <u>is not</u> going.

She <u>isn't</u> going.

➤ Rewrite the sentences with contractions.

**1.** I had not gone a step when I heard a strange buzzing.

_____

**2.** I turned around and could not believe my eyes.

_____

**3.** I did not know it was going to snow all day long.

_____

**4.** I was not prepared for my math exam today.

_____

**5.** You are not going to the movie unless you finish your homework.

_____

**6.** I could not stand sitting inside until the rain stopped.

_____

**7.** You have not seen your big sister for a long time.

_____

**8.** I would not want to take a test like that again.

_____

**9.** There is not a place to put the computer.

_____

Student
Handbook

Name _____ Date _____

## Use a Cluster Map to Write a Description

You can use a cluster map to brainstorm ideas for writing.

**A.** ➤ Think about a place in the future. Then fill in the cluster map.
Use details that relate to the five senses.

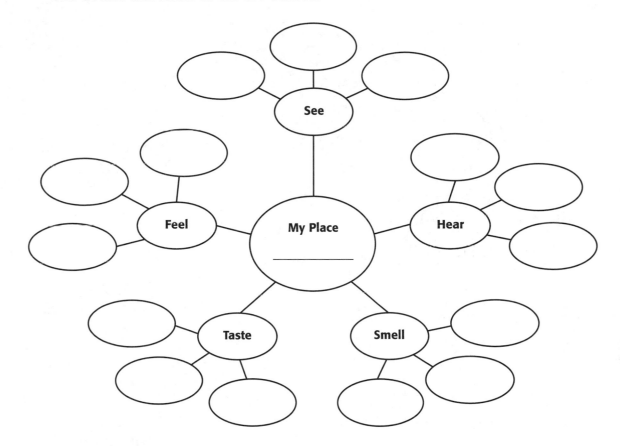

**B.** ➤ Write a paragraph that describes your place of the future.
Use the information from the cluster map.

_____

_____

_____

_____

_____

_____

_____

## Across Content Areas

Use with student text page 191.

### Read a Time Zone Map

   It is never the same time in New York City as it is in Los Angeles. That is because both cities are in different **time zones.** The United States (not counting Alaska and Hawaii) covers four time zones: Eastern, Central, Mountain, and Pacific.

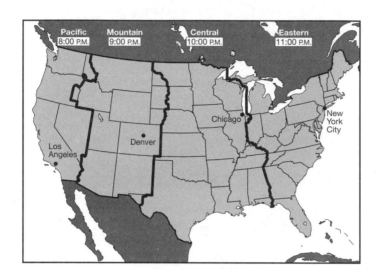

➤ Answer the questions. Use the map.

**1.** How many hours separate New York City and Los Angeles?

_____

**2.** How many hours separate New York City and Chicago?

_____

**3.** How many hours separate New York City and the town you live in?

_____

**4.** What time is it in Denver if it is 1:00 P.M. in Chicago?

_____

**5.** What time and day is it in New York City if it is 11:00 P.M. on a Monday in Los Angeles?

_____

# Build Vocabulary

*Use with student text page 193.*

## Identify Analogies

An **analogy** is a situation or relationship that is similar to another situation or relationship. Look at this analogy. It shows how a lake and the mind are similar.

As a lake holds water, a mind holds knowledge.

➤ Read the words and definitions in the box. Then complete each analogy.

---

**Word and Definition**

**vast**  large

**distance**  the space between two points

**fireflies**  insects that light up

**assume**  believe something is true

**accelerate**  increase speed

**calculation**  math

**round trip**  a journey that starts and ends in the same place

---

1. As a tunnel is narrow, _____ is vast.
   - **a.** a street
   - **b.** a staircase
   - **c.** space
   - **d.** a yard

2. As weight can be measured in grams, distance can be measured in _____.
   - **a.** seconds
   - **b.** kilograms
   - **c.** maps
   - **d.** kilometers

3. As eagles are types of birds, fireflies are types of _____.
   - **a.** fish
   - **b.** dogs
   - **c.** insects
   - **d.** mammals

4. As doubt relates to question, assume relates to _____.
   - **a.** disbelief
   - **b.** distrust
   - **c.** fact
   - **d.** opinion

5. As decelerate relates to slower, accelerate relates to _____.
   - **a.** faster
   - **b.** increase
   - **c.** decrease
   - **d.** speed

6. As organization relates to words, calculation relates to _____.
   - **a.** letters
   - **b.** numbers
   - **c.** phrases
   - **d.** formulas

7. As cycle relates to process, round trip relates to _____.
   - **a.** wheel
   - **b.** travel
   - **c.** circle
   - **d.** vacation

# Writing: Capitalization

Use with student text page 200.

## Capitalize Space Words

When writing about space, it is important to know which words are capitalized. Follow the rules listed in the chart.

| Rule | Example |
|---|---|
| The names of specific bodies in space should be capitalized. | • Mercury (the name of a planet)<br>• Io (the name of a moon)<br>• Proxima Centauri (the name of a star)<br>• Leo (the name of a constellation) |
| Names of spacecraft are capitalized. They are also italicized. The names of space programs are capitalized but not italicized. | • *Sputnik II*<br>• Project Apollo |
| Earth, Sun, and Moon (only Earth's moon) are capitalized when referring to specific names of bodies in our solar system. | • We should protect Earth's resources.<br>• The Moon orbits Earth.<br>• Earth orbits the Sun. |

Do not capitalize types of bodies in space or types of spacecraft.

That <u>planet</u> has two <u>moons</u>.

They traveled in a <u>space shuttle</u>.

The word *earth* is not capitalized when referring to the ground or soil. The word *moon* is not capitalized when referring to moons other than Earth's. The word *sun* is not capitalized when referring to suns outside of our solar system.

➤ Edit these sentences. Find the capitalization errors and rewrite each sentence. The first one has been done for you.

1. The *voyager* spacecraft explored the outer Planets of our solar system.

   *The Voyager spacecraft explored the outer planets of our solar system.*

2. We learned a lot about jupiter, saturn, uranus, and neptune.

   _____

3. The Spacecraft did not fly near pluto.

   _____

4. Cameras and computers showed us the Planets' Moons and Rings.

   _____

5. We see little of them from earth because they are far away.

   _____

## Elements of Literature

*Use with student text page 201.*

### Analyze Organization and Presentation of Ideas: Compare and Contrast

Sometimes authors compare and contrast information to show how ideas are related. Read these sentences.

If Earth were the size of a basketball, the Moon would be the size of a softball about ten steps away.

Earth and Moon are both bodies in our solar system. However, Earth is larger than the Moon.

➤ Read the passages. Then complete the Venn Diagrams to compare and contrast details.

Sari and Sam are twin sister and brother. They were born on the same day. However, Sari is a girl, and Sam is a boy. Sari and Sam both have brown hair and brown eyes. Sam is a little taller than Sari. Sam likes the arts. He enjoys drawing and writing poetry. Sari is very active. She enjoys sports. She also likes math. Both Sari and Sam are funny and kind people.

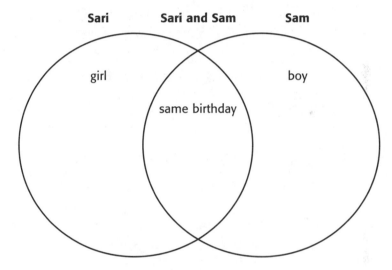

Kyle has two pets named Enzo and Lucy. They are both three years old. Enzo is a Persian cat with long, brown hair. Lucy is a Labrador dog with short, brown hair. Enzo sheds a lot of hair all over the house. However, Lucy sheds very little hair. Enzo does not like to play much. He keeps to himself and likes to sleep by the window. However, Lucy is very playful. She loves other animals and people. She loves to go to the park to run and play catch.

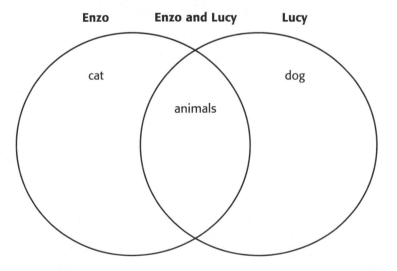

VISIONS Unit 3 • Chapter 4 Why We Can't Get There From Here

# Word Study

Use with student text page 202.

## Write Using the Suffix -est

A **suffix** is a group of letters that is added to the end of a word. A suffix may change the meaning of the word. You can use the meanings of a word and a suffix to guess the meaning of the new word.

The suffix -est means "the most of its kind." It is added to adjectives. An adjective that ends in -est is called a **superlative adjective.** Examples are: *hard—hardest, easy—easiest, hot—hottest, and close—closest.* Note these rules for spelling changes:

---

**Spelling Changes**

- The letter *y* changes to an *i* before adding -est. (*easy—easiest*)

- Double the final consonant before adding -est if a word has one syllable and ends in a short vowel + a consonant. (*hot—hottest*)

- A word ending in *e* drops the *e* before adding -est. (*close—closest*)

---

Some adjectives are irregular. They must be memorized. For example: *far—farthest, good—best, bad—worst.*

➤ Fill in the chart. Use the correct form of each superlative adjective. The first one has been done for you.

| Adjective | Superlative Adjective |
|---|---|
| **1.** fast | fastest |
| **2.** cold | |
| **3.** noisy | |
| **4.** strange | |
| **5.** dark | |
| **6.** lonely | |
| **7.** starry | |
| **8.** big | |
| **9.** empty | |
| **10.** bold | |

# Grammar Focus

*Use with student text page 202.*

## Use Superlative Adjectives

You usually form the superlative form of short adjectives by adding *-est* to the adjective. Short adjectives have one syllable or two syllables ending in *-y*.

Many adjectives are longer than two syllables. In this case, you form the superlative by adding *the most* to the adjective.

| Adjective | Long Adjective |
|---|---|
| terrible | the most terrible |
| experienced | the most experienced |
| challenged | the most challenged |

**A.** ➤ Fill in the chart. Use the correct form of each superlative adjective.

| Adjective | Short Adjective | Adjective | Long Adjective |
|---|---|---|---|
| **1.** tall | the tallest | **2.** wonderful | the most wonderful |
| **3.** warm | | **4.** capable | |
| **5.** high | | **6.** amazing | |
| **7.** low | | **8.** surprising | |

**B.** ➤ Underline the correct form of the adjective in each sentence.

1. The (excitingest/most exciting) thing happened to me last year.

2. My family went to Florida on the (goodest/best) vacation that we had ever taken.

3. We watched the (interestingest/most interesting) thing I had ever seen—a space shuttle launch.

4. Even my little sister was at her (quietest/most quiet).

5. The blastoff was the (loudest/most loud) thing I ever heard.

6. When it was over, we went to the (greatest/most great) place to eat in the world.

# Grammar Focus

*Use with student text page 202.*

## Use Comparative and Superlative Adjectives

**Superlative adjectives** are used to compare three or more things. **Comparative adjectives** are used to compare two things. To form the comparative of a short adjective add *-er* to the adjective.

Use comparative and superlative adjectives to make your writing more precise. Look at the example.

**Not Vivid and Precise:** Ben is young. Sheila is young. Lisa is young.

**More Vivid and Precise :** Ben is <u>younger</u> than Sheila. Lisa is the <u>youngest</u>.

**A.** ➤ Edit these sentences. Find the errors in comparative and superlative adjectives and rewrite each sentence. The first one has been done for you.

1. Do you wonder which of Mars's two moons is biggest?

   *Do you wonder which of Mars's two moons is bigger?*  _____

2. The astronaut is one of the more brave people in the world.

   _____

3. Venus is more close to the Sun than Earth. Mercury is the closer of all the planets.

   _____

4. I think space travel is the more fascinating topic in this book.

   _____

**B.** ➤ Write three sentences about a place you have visited. Use superlative adjectives to make your writing more precise.

1. _____

2. _____

3. _____

Student
Handbook

# From Reading to Writing

*Use with student text page 203.*

## Draft a Research Report

Use this model to help you draft the three paragraphs of your research report. Your report should have an introduction, a body, and a conclusion.

```
Title _____

        Introduction
  • Tell readers what your report is about.
  • Tell readers why the topic is interesting.

            Body
  • Include important ideas about the topic.
  • Support important ideas with details,
    examples, and facts.

         Conclusion
  • Summarize the information in the body.
  • Use different words to remind readers
    why the topic is interesting.
```

➤ Use the checklist to edit the research report you wrote in Chapter 4.

**Edit and Revise Your Report**

Title of research report: _____

**What I did:**

_____ 1. I included a title.

_____ 2. I indented each paragraph.

_____ 3. I wrote my ideas in a logical order.

_____ 4. I used details, facts, and examples to support
important ideas.

_____ 5. I corrected all errors in spelling, capitalization,
and punctuation.

# Across Content Areas

*Use with student text page 203.*

## Use Audio-Visual Resources

You can use many audiovisual resources in a presentation. Look at the audiovisual resources listed. Tell how you could use each one in a presentation about space exploration.

 **1. Audio CDs and audiocassettes** let you hear text or music.

How could you use audio CDs and audiocassettes in a presentation about space exploration?

_____

 **2. Videos** let you see moving pictures and hear sound.

How could you use videos in a presentation about space exploration?

_____

 **3. The Internet** lets you research a wide range of information.

How could you use the Internet in a presentation about space exploration?

_____

 **4. Photographs and drawings** show pictures.

How could you use photographs and drawings in a presentation about space exploration?

_____

 **5. Diagrams and charts** organize information.

How could you use diagrams and charts in a presentation about space exploration?

_____

 **6. CD-ROMs** can include video, sound, text, pictures, maps, and charts to show information on a computer.

How could you use CD-ROMs in a presentation about space exploration?

_____

# Build Vocabulary

Use with student text page 205.

## Identify Homophones

**Homophones** are words that are pronounced the same, and may have different spellings, but have different meanings. For example, the words *they're, there,* and *their* are homophones.

The chart shows some homophones and their meanings.

| Homophone 1 | Meaning | Homophone 2 | Meaning |
|---|---|---|---|
| sail | travel by boat | sale | the exchanging of things for money |
| rode | past tense of *ride* | road | a street |
| feet | body parts attached to the lower leg | feat | an act that shows great ability |
| days | the period between sunrise and sunset | daze | an unclear or shocked state |
| need | desire or want something | knead | press with the fingers and hands |
| sight | something that is seen | site | area or place |

➤ Underline the correct word in each sentence.

1. The tourists decided to (sail/sale) to the island.

2. Jessica lives on the main (rode/road) in her town.

3. My job required me to perform a great (feet/feat).

4. My cousins visited us. They stayed at our house for seven (days/daze).

5. The artists (need/knead) the clay to make beautiful pots.

6. I love the (sight/site) of autumn leaves changing color.

# Writing: Punctuation

Use with student text page 214.

## Use Commas

Some sentences include a list of more than two words joined by *and* or *or*. **Commas ( , )** are used to separate these words. Use a final comma before *and* or *or*.

We made <u>red, white, and blue</u> decorations.

Choose one activity: <u>football, soccer, or volleyball</u>.

Some sentences include a list of two words joined by *and* or *or*. In this case, a comma is not used to separate the words.

We visited <u>Paris and London</u>.

I can't decide whether I should visit <u>Ron or Gina</u>.

**A.** ➤ Add commas to the lists of items that need them.

1. breakfast**,** lunch**,** and dinner

2. James María Vince and Luis

3. movies or music

4. Italian French and Spanish

5. roses and tulips

**B.** ➤ Edit these sentences. Rewrite each sentence correcting the use of commas.

1. Henry entered the dining room carrying a bag, and a hat.

   *Henry entered the dining room carrying a bag and a hat.*

2. His clothes were old dusty and torn.

   _____

3. Everyone in the room was a prospector a peddler or a shopkeeper.

   _____

4. Henry ate a simple meal of meat potatoes gravy and bread.

   _____

5. Daisy Yuri and Joe looked at each other while Henry ate.

   _____

6. After Henry left, Joe said, "He was either a miner, or, a visitor."

   _____

# Elements of Literature

Use with student text page 215.

## Analyze Character Traits and Motivation

**Traits** tell you what a character is like. **Motivation** is the reason why a character does something. Writers often use details to help readers guess this information.

> Angela worked day and night to provide for her family. On the weekends, she tried to find time to read her favorite books.

The details help you understand that Angela is a hard worker and likes to read. You can also guess that Angela works hard because she cares for her family.

➤ Read the paragraph. Then fill in the chart.

Juan hopes to be a journalist some day. He watches several news programs every day. He likes to make up his own news stories and write them down. He even draws detailed pictures for his stories. Most of his classmates do not like to give oral presentations, but Juan does. He often asks his teacher if he can share his news stories. Juan believes that the news can be used to help people. So, he tries to share stories about good things that happen. He wants his classmates to feel good about life. One day, he finished presenting a story. His teacher said, "Juan, you have a gift for sharing news stories." Juan replied, "I get that gift from my father. He is a great journalist. I am very proud of him."

| Juan's Traits | Juan's Motivations |
|---|---|
| • likes the news | • wants to be a journalist |
| | |

**VISIONS Unit 3 • Chapter 5** The California Gold Rush and Dame Shirley and the Gold Rush

# Word Study

*Use with student text page 202.*

## Learn Words from Context and Experience

Sometimes writers do not directly tell you what a word means. However, you can often use context clues to understand new words.

You also use your own experience to understand a text. You can make connections between what is in the text and what you know.

**A.** ➤ Circle the correct definition of each underlined word. Use context clues and your experience to help you.

1. In the 1800s, many families moved west in <u>wagons</u>.
   **a.** four-wheeled vehicles pulled by animals
   **b.** fast trains

2. <u>Maladies</u> such as broken bones and illness struck wagon train members.
   **a.** sicknesses
   **b.** expenses

3. Often the wagon was <u>laden</u> with so many household goods and food that there was no place to ride.
   **a.** organized
   **b.** loaded

4. <u>Sketchy</u> maps of the unknown land were difficult to read.
   **a.** detailed
   **b.** unclear, incomplete

5. It is no wonder that many <u>prospectors</u> heading to California during the Gold Rush went by boat.
   **a.** people searching for gold
   **b.** inventors

6. The <u>maritime</u> journey was not much easier than the overland route.
   **a.** related to the sea
   **b.** a large ship

7. We should be thankful to those <u>hardy</u> people for settling the West.
   **a.** strong, able to survive difficult conditions
   **b.** fearful

8. It is difficult to imagine the hardships they <u>endured</u>.
   **a.** worked
   **b.** suffered, went through

# Grammar Focus

Use with student text page 216.

## Identify Adverbs

**Adverbs** are words that describe verbs. Adverbs can answer the questions *How?* or *How was it done?*

How did you sleep? I slept <u>poorly</u>.

How did you eat? I ate <u>quickly</u>.

How did you sing? I sang <u>sweetly</u>.

Most adverbs are formed by adding *-ly* to adjectives. If an adjective ends in *y*, change the *y* to an *i* before adding *-ly (hungry—hungrily; happy—happily).*

**A.** ➤ Fill in the chart. Use the correct form of the adverb.

| Adjective | Adverb |
|---|---|
| easy | |
| wonderful | |
| dangerous | |
| safe | |
| nervous | |
| sad | |
| brave | |
| tired | |

**B.** ➤ Complete the sentences. Use the adverbs from the chart. The first one has been done for you.

1. The test was not at all difficult. I finished it _____*easily*_____.

2. The soldiers fought _____ in battle.

3. "I am afraid to go alone," he said _____.

4. Gabby _____ stated that she needed to sleep.

5. Buckle your seat belt and drive _____.

6. She cried as she _____ told us that her cat had run away.

# Grammar Focus

*Use with student text page 202.*

## Use Adverbs for Vivid Writing

Adverbs can make a piece of writing vivid, precise, and interesting. They help readers form pictures in their mind.

**A.** ➤ Complete the paragraph. Use the adverbs from the box to make the paragraph more vivid.

| Adverbs | |
|---|---|
| warmly | dreamily |
| patiently | seriously |
| finally | wearily |
| immediately | sadly |
| loudly | |

I waited _____ for my father to come home. He walked in _____ with a heavy sack on his back. It was the last of the supplies we needed for our trip west. We were leaving _____ for Independence, Missouri. From there, we would travel to San Francisco, California. I shouted _____ at my little sister to hurry up. She was _____ saying good-bye to all the plants and birds around our house. I thought _____ about what life would be like in San Francisco. I am sure my father was thinking _____ about his new work in a mining camp. My mother bundled us _____ into the wagon. We were _____ on our way.

**B.** ➤ Write a four-sentence paragraph about a taking a trip. Use adverbs to make your writing vivid.

_____

_____

_____

Student Handbook

VISIONS C  Activity Book • Copyright © Heinle

Name _____  Date _____

○ # From Reading to Writing

*Use with student text page 217.*

**Compare and Contrast Two Characters**

Compare and contrast the characters in "The California Gold Rush" and "Dame Shirley and the Gold Rush." Fill in the Venn Diagram to help you.

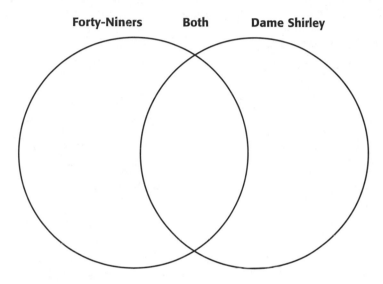

**Forty-Niners**   **Both**   **Dame Shirley**

● ➤ Write a paragraph to summarize the information in the Venn Diagram. Follow these steps.

1. Begin by telling which characters you are comparing and contrasting. Then tell which selections they are from.

2. Write one or two sentences to explain how the characters are similar. Then write one or two sentences to explain how they are different.

3. Use at least two adverbs to make your writing vivid.

4. Indent your paragraph.

_____

_____

_____

_____

_____

_____

_____

●

_____

_____

# Across Content Areas

Use with student text page 217.

## Learn About Natural Resources

➤ Read this article about natural resources.

**Natural Resources**

Nature gives us many of the things we need to live. These things are called **natural resources.** People use natural resources for food, clothing, shelter, and enjoyment. There are two groups of natural resources: renewable resources and nonrenewable resources.

**Renewable Resources**

Nature can replace the **renewable resources** we use. Some renewable resources are trees and soil. People use trees to make paper. The trees in a forest protect animals and help clean our air. People use soil to grow crops and other plants.

**Nonrenewable Resources**

Nature cannot replace **nonrenewable resources** after people use them. Some nonrenewable resources are coal, oil, limestone, gold, and other minerals. Oil is used to make gas (a fuel for cars) and to heat our homes. Coal is also used for heating. It is used to provide electricity, too. Limestone and coal are used to make steel. Then steel is used to build cars, buildings, and many other things. People can use gold to make jewelry and coins.

**A.** ➤ Fill in the chart. Use the information in the article. The first row has been done for you.

| Natural Resource | Type of Resource | How It Can Be Used |
|---|---|---|
| tree | renewable | to make paper |
| gold | | |
| coal | | |
| soil | | |

Name _____  Date _____

# Build Vocabulary

*Use with student text page 227.*

## Use Context to Understand New Words

**A.** ➤ Read the paragraph. Then match each underlined word in the paragraph to its definition.

### The Storm

Big clouds began to form before the storm. The wind was strong, and leaves flew in circles, <u>spiraling</u> up above our house. As the clouds made the sun <u>disappear</u>, everything around us <u>darkened</u>. It was like night was falling. Then the rain came down like someone had turned on a hose. It splashed off the roof and <u>cascaded</u> over the gutter. There was a pot on our back step that filled up very fast. I watched the pot <u>overflow</u> in less than a minute! But almost as quickly as it started, the rain stopped. Before long, the clouds moved apart, and we watched the sun <u>reappear</u>. The sunlight covered the wet sidewalks. My little brother ran outside and said, "Look at our street. It <u>sparkles</u>!"

### Definitions

1. _____*reappear*_____ come back into sight

2. _____ twisting up and down

3. _____ gives off bits of light

4. _____ flow over the edge of something

5. _____ go out of sight

6. _____ flowed down, as from one step to another

7. _____ became dark or dim; lost light

### Complete Sentences

**B.** ➤ Match each phrase with one of the phrases in the box to make a sentence.

1. The burning candles _____.

2. The bright lightning flashed _____.

3. The stuffed drawer _____.

4. When nighttime ends _____.

5. The winding staircase _____.

6. The bathtub filled up and _____.

7. I helped Linda find _____.

| Phrases |
| --- |
| **a.** cascaded to the floor |
| **b.** the sun reappears |
| **c.** made the dinner table sparkle |
| **d.** overflowed with clothes |
| **e.** her dog that disappeared |
| **f.** across the darkened sky |
| **g.** spiraled to the bottom floor |

# Writing: Capitalization and Punctuation

Use with student text page 234.

## Capitalize and Punctuate Sentences

A sentence usually begins with a capital (big) letter. A sentence can end with different types of punctuation (marks used in writing).

| Type of Sentence | When Sentence Is Used | Example of Sentence | Punctuation at End of Sentence |
|---|---|---|---|
| Statement | to tell information | I will talk to you soon. | **.** Period |
| Question | to ask for an answer to something | Where is the library? | **?** Question Mark |
| Exclamation | to show strong emotion or great interest | I am so happy to see you! | **!** Exclamation Point |

**A.** ➤ Complete the sentences. Use the correct punctuation mark.

**1.** Be careful ___  **2.** When are we going to leave ___  **3.** I rode my bike to the park ___

## Capitalize and Punctuate Sentences

In "Water Dance," each sentence begins with a capital letter and ends with a period. Here is the first stanza of "Water Dance." It contains four sentences.

**Sentence 1:** Some people say that I am one thing.

**Sentence 2:** Others say that I am many.

**Sentence 3:** Ever since the world began
I have been moving in an endless circle.

**Sentence 4:** Sometimes I fall from the sky.

**B.** ➤ Edit this paragraph by adding periods and capital letters.

sometimes I cascade. I tumble down, down, over the moss-covered rocks, through the forest shadows I am the mountain stream. at the foot of the mountains, I leap from a stone cliff

_____

_____

_____

_____

VISIONS Unit 4 • Chapter 1 Water Dance

VISIONS C Activity Book • Copyright © Heinle

## Elements of Literature

*Use with student text page 235.*

### Identify Images

Poets often use words that help readers create **images** (pictures) in their mind. These words often help readers connect to their senses.

I walked inside the store and felt like I had just walked inside a refrigerator.

We know the store is cold because it is compared to the inside of a refrigerator. The word *refrigerator* helps us connect to our sense of touch.

**A.** ➤ Next to each word, write the sense that it helps you connect to: sight, hearing, smell, taste, or touch.

**1.** smoky-smelling _____

**2.** freezing _____

**3.** sweet _____

**4.** booming _____

**5.** shining _____

**B.** ➤ Fill in the chart. List each word under the sense to which you connect it.

| warm | echoing | peppery | banging |
| sour | shadows | sparkles | mouth-burning |
| wet | darkened | cool | ringing |

| Sight | Touch | Hearing | Taste |
|---|---|---|---|
| shadows | | | |
| | | | |
| | | | |
| | | | |

## Word Study

*Use with student text page 236.*

### Distinguish Denotative and Connotative Meanings

Many words have more than one meaning. One meaning may be **denotative** (the exact meaning of a word).

Another meaning may give you a feeling or help you form pictures in your mind. This is called the **connotative** meaning of the word.

**A.** ➤ Write the type of meaning from the chart next to each sentence.

| Words | Denotative Meaning | Connotative Meaning |
|---|---|---|
| **veils** | pieces of cloth that cover the face | things that screen or hide |
| **golden** | made of gold | having a glowing gold color |
| **tumble** | trip and fall | roll end over end |

1. I watched the stream's water <u>tumble</u> down over moss-covered rocks.
   *connotative definition*

2. Many people wear <u>golden</u> rings on their fingers. _____

3. She bought two hats with lace <u>veils</u> for each of her daughters. _____

4. The mist rose into the air in white-silver <u>veils</u> that covered the sun.

   _____

5. When I caught my foot on the stair, it made me <u>tumble</u> onto my knees.

   _____

6. The rivers wind through <u>golden</u> valleys, joined by streams and creeks.

   _____

**B.** ➤ Complete each sentence with the correct word from the chart.

1. Her light brown hair turned _____ from the summer sun.

2. The soccer balls _____ down the porch stairs and into yard.

3. The king drank from a _____ cup.

4. The firemen walked through _____ of smoke.

5. I am afraid I will _____ on the slippery ice.

6. Some women wear _____ over their face when they get married.

VISIONS C Activity Book • Copyright © Heinle

Name _____ Date _____

# Grammar Focus

Use with student text page 236.

## Use Comparative and Superlative Adjectives

The ending -er can be added to short adjectives to make **comparative adjectives.** They compare two things.

A rabbit is <u>fast</u>. An antelope is <u>fast**er**</u> than a rabbit.

The ending -est can be added to short adjectives to make **superlative adjectives.** They compare three or more things.

A rabbit is <u>fast</u>. An antelope is <u>fast**er**</u> than a rabbit. A cheetah is the <u>fast**est**</u> of all land animals.

Note that if an adjective ends in the letter *y*, the *y* is replaced by an *i* when -er or -est are added. For example:

The problem is <u>easy</u>. The second problem is <u>eas**i**er</u>. The third problem is <u>eas**i**est</u>.

**A.** ➤ Fill in the chart. Use the comparative and superlative forms of the adjectives listed.

| Base Word | Comparative Form | Superlative Form |
|---|---|---|
| heavy | heavi**er** | heavi**est** |
| deep | | |
| wide | | |
| high | | |
| funny | | |

**B.** ➤ Complete each sentence. Add -er or -est to each underlined adjective to make the comparative or superlative form.

1. My room is <u>neat</u>, but my sister's room is _____*neater*_____. Mom's room is the _____*neatest*_____.

2. It starts to get <u>cold</u> in November. December is _____, and January is the _____ month.

3. Pikes Peak is a <u>high</u> mountain, but Denali Peak is _____. Mt. Everest is the _____ in the world.

4. Stores are <u>busy</u> at different times of the year. The _____ holiday for most stores is Christmas.

5. Some people feel <u>happy</u> when they see the sun rise. Which makes you _____, the morning, the evening, or the middle of the day?

# Build Vocabulary

*Use with student text page 236.*

## Use Superlative Adjectives to Clarify Meaning

We can use superlative adjectives to make the meaning of sentences clearer. For example, read these sentences:

The music was <u>loud</u>, but the fireworks were <u>louder</u>. The thunder was <u>louder</u>.

Even though the sentences make sense, the meaning is not as clear as it could be. Using the superlative ending *-est* makes the meaning clear:

The music was <u>loud</u>, but the fireworks were <u>louder</u>. The thunder was <u>loudest</u>.

➤ Write sentences using the adjectives to compare the things listed. Use superlative adjectives to make your writing precise.

1. <u>soft</u>          kitten, towel, pillow

_____

_____

_____

2. <u>easy</u>          walking, running, sitting

_____

_____

_____

3. <u>deep</u>          ocean, pond, lake

_____

_____

_____

4. <u>quiet</u>          mouse, cat, snake

_____

_____

_____

5. <u>large</u>          camel, elephant, whale

_____

_____

_____

# From Reading to Writing

**Edit a Poem**

*Use with student text page 237.*

➤ Use the checklist to edit the poem you wrote in Chapter 1.

**Editing Checklist for a Poem**

Title of poem: _____

**What I did:**

_____ **1.** I chose something I like. The ideas I brainstormed were:

_____

_____

_____

_____ **2.** I used figurative language. One example I used is:

_____

_____

_____

_____ **3.** I used comparative adjectives. The three things I compared were:

_____

_____

_____

_____ **4.** I followed the model to help me write my poem.

_____ **5.** I read the poem aloud to evaluate how it sounded.

## Across Content Areas

Use with student text page 238.

### Understand Graphic Presentations

Look at this graphic presentation and the information about the water cycle.

**The Water Cycle**

Look at the picture. It shows the steps in the water cycle. The water cycle on Earth has three steps: **evaporation**, **condensation**, and **precipitation**.

**Evaporation**

**Evaporation** happens on the surface of Earth where there is water. When water evaporates, it turns from a liquid into a gas.

**Condensation**

As the evaporated water rises into the air, it begins to cool. High up in the air, the water condenses, or starts to come together, from a gas into a liquid. **Condensation** of water forms the clouds. Clouds are made of tiny droplets of water and ice so small that they can float on air. Wind moves the clouds across the sky.

**Precipitation**

The water droplets and tiny pieces of ice join together to form larger drops of ice crystals. Eventually, the crystals become too heavy to float on the air. The water then falls back to Earth as **precipitation.** If the air near the ground is cold enough, the water falls as snow, sleet, or ice. If the air near the ground is warm, the water falls as rain. Most precipitation falls onto the oceans, but some falls onto land and evaporates again. Some runs into streams and rivers. Water moves over Earth's surface and through the ground. Finally, it reaches the oceans.

The cycle continues as water from the land and oceans evaporates, condenses in the atmosphere, and falls to Earth's surface again as precipitation.

➤ Answer the questions. Use the article and glossary.

1. What is this article about?

_____

2. Why is the process of evaporation, condensation, and precipitation of water called the "water cycle"?

_____

3. You want to learn how water returns to the oceans. Where in the diagram would you look?

_____

**128**

Name _____  Date _____

# Build Vocabulary
## Use Synonyms and Antonyms

*Use with student text page 239.*

Words that have similar meanings are called **synonyms**. *Happy* and *glad* are synonyms. Words that have opposite meanings are called **antonyms**. *Happy* and *sad* are antonyms.

**Find Synonyms and Antonyms**

**A.** ➤ Write *synonym* or *antonym* for each pair of words.

1. happy : sad  _____ *antonyms*
2. empty : full  _____
3. closed : shut  _____
4. first : last  _____

**B.** ➤ Find the synonym or antonym. Use the words in the box.

| Word | Definition |
|---|---|
| harvests | gathers crops |
| messenger | person who brings news or messages |
| begged | asked as if for a favor |
| roared | shouted very loudly or angrily |
| reasonable | referring to the right thing to do |
| swallowed | ate |
| searched | looked for |

1. Find a synonym for <u>collects</u>.  _____ *harvests*
2. Find a synonym for <u>hunted</u>.  _____
3. Find a synonym for <u>whispered</u>.  _____
4. Find a synonym for <u>reporter</u>.  _____
5. Find a synonym for <u>spit out</u>.  _____
6. Find a synonym for <u>unfair</u>.  _____
7. Find a synonym for <u>pleaded</u>.  _____

# Writing: Capitalization

*Use with student text page 246.*

## Capitalize Proper Nouns

A noun refers to a person, a place, or a thing, for example, *player, city,* and *peace.* A **proper noun** names a specific person, place, or thing. Proper nouns are always capitalized. Look at these examples:

**J**ason **R**amirez, **Y**ellowstone **N**ational **P**ark, **L**incoln **S**chool, **P**resident **W**ashington, **S**arah **B**ernhardt.

Here is a sentence from "Persephone and the Seasons." The proper nouns in the sentence are underlined.

"<u>Pluto</u> must let <u>Persephone</u> leave the <u>Underworld</u>," said a goddess. "Only then will <u>Demeter</u> save the <u>Earth</u>."

**A.** ➤ Read the list of nouns. Find the four proper nouns and write them on the lines. Remember to begin each proper noun with a capital letter.

| **Nouns** | | | |
| --- | --- | --- | --- |
| paperweight | atlantic ocean | fairness | school |
| sailor | baseball | texas | theater |
| mount rushmore | george washington | | |

1. _____

2. _____

3. _____

4. _____

**B.** ➤ Edit this paragraph. Make sure that each proper noun begins with a capital letter. Underline the errors.

"Persephone and the Seasons" is a Greek myth. People in ancient Greece and ancient rome told many of the same stories, but they often gave different names to the gods and goddesses in their myths. For example, the king of the gods in Greek myths is zeus, but in Roman myths he is called jupiter. The messenger of the gods was hermes to the greeks and Mercury to the romans. A few names were the same, though. In the myths of both greece and Rome, the sun god is named apollo.

## Elements of Literature

*Use with student text page 247.*

**React to the Theme**

The **theme** is the main idea or meaning of a piece of writing. The theme of "Persephone and the Seasons" is nature and the change of seasons.

People told this story to compare and contrast winter and summer. It also helped them express different feelings they had about the seasons.

Compare and contrast your feelings about winter and summer. Write what you like and do not like about each season. Then write what you like and do not like about each season.

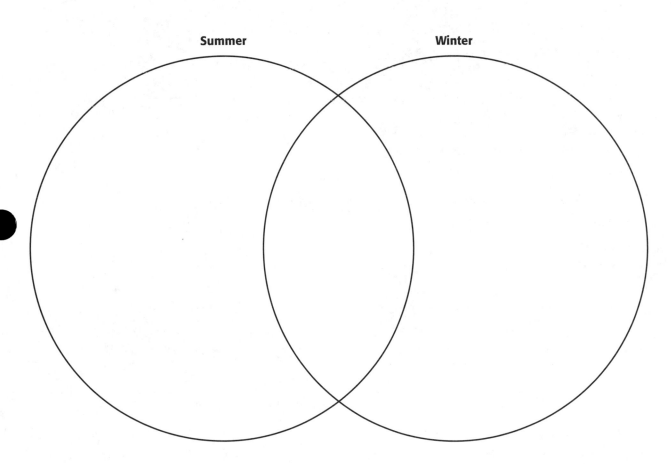

**Summer**          **Winter**

# Word Study

*Use with student text page 248.*

## Recognize Contractions

A negative sentence often has the word *not*.

We <u>are</u> **not** <u>going</u> to the movies tomorrow.

Contractions are often made with auxiliary verbs like *does, have,* and *should* and the word *not*. The letter *o* is dropped from *not* and replaced by an apostrophe ( **'** ).

| Full Forms | Contractions |
|---|---|
| does not | doesn't |
| have not | haven't |
| should not | shouldn't |

➤ Complete the sentences. Use the words in the box to make contractions. The first one has been done for you.

```
are not
did not
were not
was not
could not
```

1. The stone was too heavy to lift. I _____*couldn't*_____ move it.

2. It _____ Tim's turn, so he waited in his seat until it was.

3. Maria and Connie _____ going to be able to go to the fair tomorrow.

4. No one could reach the ball. Our arms _____ long enough.

5. The plants on Earth _____ grow while Demeter searched for her daughter.

# Grammar Focus

*Use with student text page 248.*

## Write Using Irregular Past Tense Verbs

**Past tense verbs** describe actions that happened in the past. For most regular verbs, you form the past tense by adding *-ed* to the verb. For regular verbs that end in "e," drop the "e" and add *-ed*.

| Regular Present Tense | Past Tense |
| --- | --- |
| happen | happened |
| erase | erased |

Irregular verbs form their past tense forms in different ways. You must memorize the past tense forms of irregular verbs.

| Irregular Verbs | |
| --- | --- |
| **Simple Form** | **Past Tense Form** |
| break | broke |
| catch | caught |
| come | came |
| draw | drew |
| go | went |
| have | had |
| run | ran |
| sing | sang |
| teach | taught |

**A.** ➤ Complete the sentences. Use the words in the chart. The first one has been done for you.

1. **go**      We _____*went*_____ for a long walk.

2. **sing**     Yeung _____ in front of a group of people.

3. **have**     I _____ eggs for breakfast this morning.

4. **teach**    His mother _____ him how to speak Thai.

5. **come**    Who _____ to your birthday party?

**B.** ➤ Edit the paragraph. Rewrite the paragraph correcting the errors in irregular past tense verbs.

When Pluto chased Persephone, she runned away as fast as she could. But Pluto catched her and took her to the Underworld. Demeter could not find Persephone anywhere. It breaked her heart when she could not find her daughter.

_____

_____

_____

_____

_____

_____

## Build Vocabulary

*Use with student text page 248.*

### Use Irregular Past Tense Verbs in Negatives, Questions, and Contractions

To make past tense sentences negative, use the auxiliary verb *did + not* + the simple form of the verb.

| Subject | *did + not* (*didn't*) | Simple Form of Verb | Sentence |
|---|---|---|---|
| I<br>You<br>He, She, It<br>We<br>They | did not<br>didn't | run | He did not run as fast as you.<br>He didn't run as fast as you. |
| | | draw | I did not draw with pens.<br>I didn't draw with pens. |
| | | have | We did not have time.<br>We didn't have time. |

**A.** ➤ Write each sentence in the negative form. Then write each negative sentence using a contraction. The first two have been done for you.

1. I had a new bike in the garage.

   *I did not have a new bike in the garage. I didn't have a new bike in the garage.*

2. We drew a picture for our presentation.

   *We did not draw a picture for our presentation. We didn't draw a picture for our presentation.*

3. They went away on the weekend.

   _____

4. I broke two dishes while washing them.

   _____

5. She sang very loudly.

   _____

To ask a question in the past tense, use *did* + the subject + the simple form of the verb:

**Statement:** I sang a folk song.

**Question:** <u>Did</u> you <u>sing</u> a folk song?

**B.** ➤ Write a question for each statement.

**Student Handbook**

1. I caught a bad cold. _____

2. They drew from their earlier experiences. _____

3. It ran across the yard. _____

Name _____  Date _____

# From Reading to Writing

*Use with student text page 249.*

**Summarize a Story Idea**

➤ Read this summary of "Persephone and the Seasons."

> Demeter, Persephone's mother, is the goddess who cares for growing things. Pluto takes Persephone to the Underworld, and he keeps her there for half of each year. When Persephone is in the Underworld, Demeter is sad. She does not tend the earth, and leaves fall from the trees. The world becomes cold and dark, and nothing grows. When Persephone returns, Demeter is happy again. Plants begin to grow again, and the earth turns green.

➤ Now suppose that the myth ended differently. Here are three possible changes:

1. Persephone must stay in the Underworld all year long.

2. Persephone must stay in the Underworld for only three months.

3. Persephone does not have to stay in the Underworld at all.

➤ Choose a new ending for the myth. Write a summary of your ending. Use this checklist to help you.

_____ 1. I chose one of the three new endings for the myth.

_____ 2. I indented my paragraph.

_____ 3. I included the most important information.

**Summary:**

_____
_____
_____
_____
_____
_____
_____
_____

## Build Vocabulary

Use with student text page 249.

### Compare Myths from Different Cultures

Many cultures use myths in the oral tradition to explain nature. Here is an example from Vietnam.

**Why the Moon Is Pale**

Long ago, Earth was dark. The people could not see one another. Jade Emperor, the ruler of the sky, felt sorry for them. He called his beautiful daughters, Sister Sun and Sister Moon.

Jade Emperor said to Sister Sun, "Walk across the sky every day. As you walk, turn your golden face toward Earth, and give the people warmth and light." He then turned to Sister Moon and said, "Watch over the people at night and give them bright light so they may finish their work."

The people on Earth rejoiced to see Sister Sun and Sister Moon in the sky. They happily planted farms in the bright sunlight. They gladly finished their work as Sister Moon shone through the darkness.

One night as Sister Moon appeared in the sky, she noticed that all the people were very tired. She hung her head in shame. She knew that her great brightness kept people from falling asleep.

"What can I do?" Sister Moon asked her parents. "I am as bright and beautiful as my sister. How can I turn my face away from the world?"

Queen Mother of the West draped a veil across Sister Moon's face. "Now," she said, "you will be able to watch over the people without disturbing their rest."

Sister Moon did not want to hide her beauty, but she agreed to wear the veil. As she appeared above Earth, the people praised her gentle beauty! They loved the soft silver light of Sister Moon as much as the warm rays of Sister Sun!

Forever after, the sisters took turns watching over the people of Earth, one during the days, and the other during the nights.

➤ Answer the questions. Use this myth and "Persephone and the Seasons."

1. Compare Jade Emperor in this myth to Zeus in "Persephone and the Seasons."

   _____

   _____

2. "Persephone and the Seasons" explains the cycle of seasons from winter to summer. What cycle does "Why the Moon Is Pale" explain?

   _____

   _____

Name _____ Date _____

● # Build Vocabulary

*Use with student text page 251.*

## Understand Words in Context and Find Words in a Dictionary

**Words in Context**

**A.** ➤ Complete the paragraph. Use the words in the box. The first one has been done for you.

---

**Word and Definition**

**adventure**  an exciting journey or event
**accompanied**  went with someone
**circuit**  something that moves in a circle
**clasped**  gripped or held tightly

**principal**  most important; the person
who directs a school
**struggled**  tried hard; made a great effort
**wearily**  in a tired way

---

Anna and Ramon _____*accompanied*_____ me to the lake near our school. We walked

in a slow _____ around the lake. The walk suddenly became a dangerous

_____!

As we crossed the bridge, a board broke. Ramon fell into the river! Worst of all,

Ramon cannot swim!

Anna dove in the water to help him. She _____ Ramon's backpack

with one hand. She used her other hand to swim while Ramon _____ to

keep his head above the water.

Anna was tired. Her arms and legs moved _____ in the water. Just

then, our teacher and school _____ splashed into the river and pulled

Anna and Ramon to safety.

**Find Words in a Dictionary**

**Guide words** are the words at the top of each dictionary page. Guide words tell you
the first and last words that are included on the page.

**B.** ➤ Write the correct word from the word box above between each pair of guide words.

<u>Guide Word</u>  <u>Guide Word</u>

1. circle _____*circuit*_____ clap

2. accept _____ admit

3. prance _____ professional

4. stop _____ style

# Writing: Punctuation

Use with student text page 260.

## Punctuate Foreign Words and Dialogue

**Punctuate Foreign Words**

In "The Circuit," the narrator's father speaks only in Spanish. Look at this sentence from the selection:

Papá sighed, wiped the sweat from his forehead with his sleeve, and said wearily, *"Es todo."*

Papá's Spanish words are printed in **italics** (*italics*). In English writing, words from other languages are often printed in italics.

**A.** ➤ Edit this paragraph. Underline each word or phrase from another language that should be in italics.

At my school, a lot of us like to say things like "hello," "goodbye," "yes," and "no" in foreign languages. My friend Anju says "bonjour" every morning. Toni likes to say "adios" when she leaves. My way of greeting people is to say "guten tag." Janice always says "yes" in Japanese, so we hear the word "hai" all day. It's really fun!

**Punctuate Dialogue with Foreign Words**

Words from other languages often appear in dialogue (the words that characters speak). The words are inside quotation marks (" ").

**B.** ➤ Write quotation marks in each sentence below.

1. *Mi olla,* she used to say proudly.

2. Yes, I like *corridos,* I answered.

Name _____  Date _____

# Elements of Literature

Use with student text page 261.

## Identify Point of View

A story's **point of view** shows who tells the story.

First-person point of view means that a character in the story is telling it. This character is called the **narrator.** First person point of view includes the words *I* and *we.*

In **third-person point of view,** the narrator is not a character in the story. The narrator uses the words *he, she, it,* and *they* and tells what the characters do, think, and feel.

| Point of View | | |
|---|---|---|
| | **Feature** | **Example** |
| FIRST-PERSON | The narrator uses the words *I* and *we.* | I listened to the song on the radio |
| THIRD-PERSON | The narrator uses the words *he, she, it,* and *they.* | He listened to the song on the radio |

**A.** ➤ Write *first* in front of the passages that are written in the first-person point of view. Write *third* in front of the passages in the third-person point of view.

1. _____ The plane landed after a long trip. I could not believe that we were finally in Hong Kong! I could not wait to see my grandparents.

2. _____ Gail wrapped her mother's birthday present carefully. She was proud of the painting she made for her. "I wonder if Mom will frame this," she thought.

3. _____ Barbara saw Carlos across the street and thought to herself, "Carlos looks happy." She waved. Carlos smiled. He waved back.

4. _____ I saw Carlos across the street. I thought he looked happy. I waved, and he smiled and waved back.

Name _____    Date _____

# Word Study

*Use with student text page 262.*

### Write Adverbs with *-ly*

**Adverbs** describe verbs. They help readers form pictures of the actions in their minds. Many adjectives can be turned into adverbs by adding *-ly*.

"Would you like to read?" he asked <u>hesitant**ly**</u>.

*Hesitant* is an adjective that can mean "slow" or "cautious." The adverb *hesitantly* tells us how the question was asked—in a slow or cautious way.

**A.** ➤ Complete the sentences. Use the adverb form of the underlined adjective.

1. His answers were always very <u>clear</u>.

   He always answered very _____.

2. When I won the match, Mom gave me a <u>proud</u> look.

   When I won the match, Mom looked at me _____.

3. It made Sheila <u>glad</u> to greet her grandmother.

   Sheila greeted her grandmother _____.

**B.** ➤ Fill in the chart. Add *-ly* to each adjective to form an adverb.
Then write its definition.

| Adjective | Definition | | Adverb | Definition |
|---|---|---|---|---|
| quick | fast | **+ -ly** | quickly | in a fast way |
| pleasant | easygoing | | | |
| sad | unhappy | | | |
| smart | intelligent | | | |
| neat | clean or tidy | | | |

VISIONS Unit 4 • Chapter 3 The Circuit

VISIONS C Activity Book • Copyright © Heinle

**140**

Name _____  Date _____

# Build Vocabulary

Use with student text page 262.

## Identify Dependent Clauses

A **dependent clause** has a subject and a verb. It cannot stand alone. Dependent clauses often begin with words like *when, after, before, as, while,* or *until* to tell when something happens.

When a dependent clause is at the beginning of a sentence, a comma comes after the clause.

<u>When the rabbit was startled,</u> it jumped into the air.

**A.** ➤ Underline the dependent clause in each sentence.

1. As long as we were at the mall, we decided to stop for lunch.

2. My sister swept the sidewalk while I cut the grass.

3. Whenever it snows, ice forms on the edge of our roof.

4. Ever since we changed the tires on my bicycle, it rides much more smoothly.

5. We go skating as soon as the ponds freeze.

**B.** ➤ Complete these sentences. For each one, choose a dependent clause from the box. Remember to capitalize the first letter of each sentence.

| |
|---|
| when you ride your bike |
| before you try them on |
| before she asks the teacher |
| when I see my grandmother |
| when you want to borrow a book |

1. She always looks up words in the dictionary _____.

2. _____, I give her a big hug.

3. _____, you should ask me for permission.

4. Be sure to wear a helmet _____.

5. Don't buy those jeans _____.

# Grammar Focus

Use with student text page 262.

## Punctuate Dependent Clauses

Even though a dependent clause includes a subject and a verb, it cannot be a sentence on its own. It needs another clause to make a complete sentence.

**A.** ➤ Mark the word groups as a dependent clause or a sentence. The first one has been done for you.

1. When Juanita left school yesterday. _____*dependent clause*_____

2. If you can not come, please let me know. _____

3. Before the game started, both teams cheered. _____

4. After it finally stopped raining. _____

5. Until I can finish my work. _____

**B.** ➤ Edit these sentences. Add the missing comma.

1. While it was raining we played a game inside.

2. When Melissa arrived the party started.

3. As long as you are up please bring me a glass of water.

4. I went to the store after I finished cleaning my room.

5. Before Manolo went to the movie he ate a sandwich.

**C.** ➤ Write complete sentences. Use the dependent clauses.

1. Before I got to school

_____

_____

2. When my dog hears thunder

_____

_____

3. While Andy was sleeping

_____

Student
Handbook

Name _____ Date _____

# From Reading to Writing

*Use with student text page 263.*

### Edit a Letter

➤ Use the checklist to edit the letter you wrote in Chapter 3.

**Editing Checklist for a Letter**

**What I did:**

_____ 1. I included my address and the date at the top of the page.

_____ 2. I included the name and address of the person I am writing to.

_____ 3. I started my letter with *Dear* _____,

_____ 4. I indented my paragraph.

_____ 5. I ended the letter with *Sincerely* and my name.

_____ 6. I corrected spelling mistakes.

_____ 7. I used resourccs such as a dictionary or the computer spell check.

_____ 8. I used a dictionary or a thesaurus to help me choose vivid words.

Some words I chose were: _____

_____

Name _____ Date _____

## Across Content Areas

*Use with student text page 263.*

### Use Internet Resources

Migrant workers move from farm to farm to help harvest food. Their work requires much travel throughout the year. For example, some migrant workers help harvest wheat. They may drive from California to Montana every year. They time their journey north so that they will arrive in each place in time for the harvest. Then they work their way back south again for a second harvest.

Research the Internet to learn more about migrant workers. Search using the keywords *migrant workers*.

URL (shows the website address)

Links (web pages you can click on to get information)

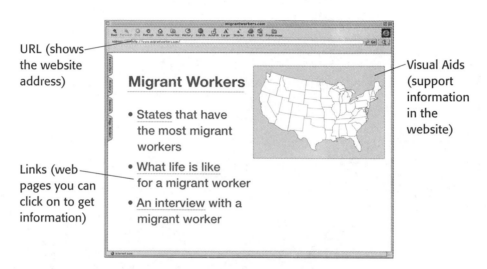

Visual Aids (support information in the website)

**Migrant Workers**

• States that have the most migrant workers

• What life is like for a migrant worker

• An interview with a migrant worker

➤ Answer the questions. Use your Internet research. If you cannot use the Internet, use other resources such as an encyclopedia or interviews with people you know.

1. In what states are the most migrant workers found?

_____

2. What kinds of jobs do migrant workers do?

_____

_____

3. What are some difficulties migrant workers face?

_____

_____

# Build Vocabulary

*Use with student text page 265.*

**Find and Use Definitions**

**Read the passage.**

> People long ago believed that all things in nature were made of only a few substances. Just 300 years ago, very few of the elements had been identified. Gradually, scientists learned that many common compounds were made of smaller parts. For example, scientists learned that water is made up of two gases, hydrogen and oxygen.
>
> Today, more than 100 elements have been identified. The process through which these discoveries were made is called "the scientific method." The scientific method is a process of steps. First, someone has an idea of how something might be explained. Then the person's theory is tested to see if its explanation is correct.

**A.** ➤ Choose the correct definition for the underlined words above.
    Use context clues in the passage.

1. **substances**
   a. matter; things
   b. important issues

2. **elements**
   a. types of weather
   b. basic substances all things are made of

3. **compounds**
   a. parts of words
   b. combinations of elements

4. **oxygen**
   a. a gas in the atmosphere that we need to breathe
   b. a metal used to make jewelry

5. **process**
   a. a series of steps
   b. a question

6. **theory**
   a. a law
   b. an idea or argument that something is true

**B.** ➤ Fill in the web. What processes can you brainstorm?

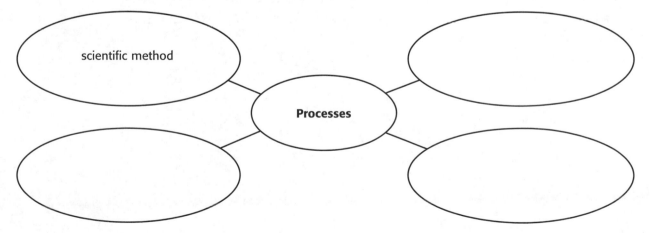

# Writing: Punctuation

*Use with student text page 272.*

## Punctuate Commas in a Series

Writers use commas to help make their writing clear. How many friends are named in the first row of the chart below? The correct answer is *five*.

| Not Correct | My best friends are Alma Ann Marie Albert Juan Carlo and Donna. |
|---|---|
| Correct | My best friends are Alma, Ann Marie, Albert, Juan Carlo, and Donna. |

Use commas only when more than two items are listed right after each other. If two items are connected by *and* or *or*, you do not need to use a comma.

I visited Ann Marie and Juan Carlo in New York.

**A.** ➤ Write need commas or do not need commas after each list. The first one has been done for you.

1. gold and silver _____ *do not need commas* _____

2. hydrogen oxygen and carbon _____

3. car truck van and boat _____

4. men women boys and girls _____

5. elements and compounds _____

**B.** ➤ Edit this paragraph. Write the missing commas in the paragraph. Cross out commas that are not necessary.

Almost everything around you is a compound. Compounds are made of combinations of elements. For example, table salt is a compound of the elements sodium, and chlorine. The material used to make paper contains the three elements carbon hydrogen and oxygen. The air we breathe has many gases in it, including nitrogen oxygen, and carbon dioxide, among other gases.

Name _____  Date _____

# Elements of Literature

*Use with student text page 273.*

## Use a Storyboard

➤ Fill in the storyboard to show the process described. In each box, draw a picture that shows a step in the process. Summarize each step on the lines.

**Grow a Plant**

Place some potting soil in a paper cup until it is half-full. Second, place some plant seeds in the cup. Third, fill the cup with more potting soil. Fourth, place the cup in a sunny place, such as a window. Next, water the soil until it is moist. Then water it once a week. Finally, check the soil every few days. After a few weeks, you should see little stems rising through the soil!

| 1. _____ | 2. _____ | 3. _____ |
|---|---|---|
|  |  |  |
| 4. _____ | 5. _____ | 6. _____ |
|  |  |  |

# Word Study

Use with student text page 274.

## Use Word Origins

Many English words come from Greek and Latin. The meanings of the English words often relate to the meanings of the words they come from.

➤ Study the word webs. Then match each Greek or Latin word in the center oval with the correct definition below. Use your knowledge of the English words to help you.

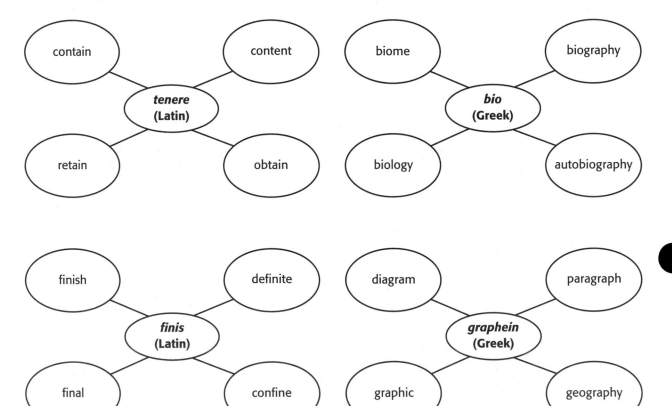

**Words**

1. _____

2. _____

3. _____

4. _____

**Definitions**

end, limit

write, draw, or describe

life

hold

# Grammar Focus

*Use with student text page 274.*

## Recognize the Active and Passive Voices

A writer can form sentences in the **active voice** or the **passive voice.** In the active voice, the subject carries out the action of the verb.

Thomas carried his books.
**Subject  →  Action**

In the passive voice, the subject receives the action of the verb.

The books were carried by Thomas.
**Subject  ←  Action**

In the passive voice sentence, *Thomas* does the action of the verb. However, the subject of the sentence is *books*. The books receive the action of the sentence.

➤ Underline the subject and the verb in each sentence. Then circle the sentences that are written in the active voice.

1. Kareem jumped higher than anyone else at the track meet.

2. We were hired by our neighbor to clean his yard.

3. The herd of cows walked slowly across the grass.

4. Alexandro threw the stick for the dog.

5. The famous singer was recognized when he walked into the restaurant.

# Grammar Focus

Use with student text page 274.

## Change Passive to Active Voice

To change an active voice sentence to a passive voice sentence, add the correct form of *be* to a past participle (a form of a verb). Look at the examples:

**Active Voice**

**Subject    Verb**

<u>Christina</u> <u>performs</u> in the leading role.

**Passive Voice**

**Subject        Past Participle**

The <u>leading role</u> is <u>performed</u> by Christina.

The passive voice sentence above includes *is,* which is the present tense form of *be.* The word *performed* is the past participle of *perform.*

➤ Rewrite the sentences. Change the active voice into the passive voice, and the passive voice into the active voice. The first one has been done for you.

1. Jason gave the most interesting gift.

   *The most interesting gift was given by Jason.*

2. My grandmother's gutters were cleaned by my father.

   _____

   _____

3. The class was warned to stay together by the principal.

   _____

   _____

4. The fox chased the rabbit.

   _____

   _____

5. Sonya's beautiful voice was admired by everyone.

Student Handbook

   _____

   _____

# From Reading to Writing

*Use with student text page 275.*

## Edit Writing Instructions

➤ Use the checklist to edit the paragraph you wrote and the diagram you created in Chapter 4.

**Editing Checklist for a Biography**

**What I did:**

_____ 1. I chose a process I know. I gave instructions for how to:

_____

_____

_____ 2. I explained the process in the first sentence.

_____ 3. I wrote the steps in the process. I wrote the steps in order. The steps are:

_____

_____

_____

_____ 4. I used transition words such as *first, next, then,* and *finally.*

_____ 5. I created a diagram for the process. I drew the diagram with:

_____

_____

_____ 6. I had a friend try to follow my instructions. I made these changes in my instructions:

_____

_____

## Across Content Areas

Use with student text page 275.

### Compare Living and Nonliving Things

You can sometimes compare the qualities of a living thing with something that is not living. Look at this example:

| Bird | Plane |
|---|---|
| 1. Uses energy to fly and stay warm | 1. Uses energy to fly |
| 2. Gets rid of waste from food | 2. Gets rid of waste from fuel |
| 3. Uses wings to fly | 3. Uses wings to fly |

➤ Fill in the chart. Compare a living thing with a nonliving thing. Write the name of each thing on the line in the top two boxes. Draw a picture of each thing below the name.

| Living Thing | Nonliving Thing |
|---|---|
| _____ | _____ |
| 1. _____ _____ _____ | 1. _____ _____ _____ |
| 2. _____ _____ _____ | 2. _____ _____ _____ |
| 3. _____ _____ _____ | 3. _____ _____ _____ |

VISIONS C  Activity Book • Copyright © Heinle

# Build Vocabulary

Use with student text page 285.

## Find Synonyms

Word that have similar meanings are called **synonyms**. The underlined words below are synonyms.

Dolphins are <u>smart</u> animals. These <u>intelligent</u> mammals have very special ways of communicating with one another.

**A.** ➤ Match the underlined word in each sentence to its synonym. Use a dictionary if you need help.

**Word in a Sentence**

**Synonym**

1. ___*b*___ Soup is a great <u>remedy</u> for treating a cold.

    **a.** honest

2. _____ Abe Lincoln was known as <u>forthright</u> because he said what he believed.

    **b.** cure

3. _____ The bus schedule has changed many times, but now it is <u>permanent</u>.

    **c.** energy

    **d.** ablaze

4. _____ The skateboarder rolled downhill quickly, gathering <u>momentum</u> as he went.

    **e.** tolerate

5. _____ People who cannot <u>endure</u> cold weather often move to warm climates.

    **f.** unchanging

6. _____ With a bit of dry wood and a flame, a campfire can be <u>ignited</u>.

## Parts of Speech: Nouns

The part of speech of a word describes how it is used. A **noun** names a person, place, or thing. In the sentence *I read a <u>book</u>,* the word *book* is a noun.

**B.** ➤ Underline the noun in each sentence.

1. Where is the <u>telephone</u>?
2. I live in a house.
3. Did you buy a car?
4. Please go to the store.
5. I found a puppy.

# Writing: Capitalization

*Use with student text page 296.*

## Capitalize Proper Nouns

**Proper nouns** name specific people, places, and things. Proper nouns are always capitalized. Words that begin sentences are also capitalized.

➤ Read these sentences from "Rosa Parks," and notice the capitalized words:

In 1931 a neighbor introduced **R**osa to **R**aymond **P**arks.
**D**ecember 1, 1955, started out like any other **T**hursday for **R**osa.
**S**he went to her job at the **M**ontgomery **F**air department store.
**O**n **D**ecember 5, 1955, **R**osa and her attorney, **F**red **G**ray, appeared before **J**udge **J**ohn **B**. **S**cott in the city court of **M**ontgomery, **A**labama.

**A.** ➤ Answer the questions. Use the sentences above. There may be more than one answer for each question.

1. Which capitalized words are parts of people's names?

   _____, *Raymond Parks*, _____, _____

2. Which capitalized words are dates?

   _____, _____

3. Which capitalized words are places?

   _____, _____

4. Which capitalized word is a title that describes someone's job?

   _____

5. Which capitalized words are parts of the name of a building?

   _____

**B.** ➤ Edit these sentences. Rewrite each sentence capitalizing all words that should be capitalized.

1. i have never lived outside of new York City.

   *I have never lived outside of New York City.*

2. have you ever visited the Empire state Building?

   _____

3. People come from as far as japan and china to see it.

   _____

4. I went to see the statue of Liberty with louis.

   _____

# Elements of Literature

## Use Description

In "Rosa Parks," the author describes characters by writing about how they act. The descriptions help readers understand why the characters act as they do.

> At her <u>new school</u> Rosa <u>learned everything</u>, from <u>how to read world maps</u> to <u>how to mix remedies</u> for sick and ailing souls. She <u>even took cooking lessons</u>.

From reading this description, the reader understands that Rosa loved to learn.

**A.** ➤ Underline the word or words that describe the people.

1. Raymond Parks was <u>smart</u>, <u>smooth talking</u>, <u>forthright</u>, and <u>persistent</u>.

2. He took a quick liking to Rosa. But she was not immediately impressed with him.

3. Raymond was well-spoken and cared deeply about the plight of black people in the South.

4. Rosa was grateful for her job.

5. It would take the force of one woman's iron will to stop racism in its tracks.

**B.** ➤ Answer the questions. Use the sentences above. The first one has been done for you.

1. How did Raymond Parks act?

   *He was intelligent, and he acted like someone who felt sure of himself.*

2. When Rosa first met Raymond, how did she react to him?

   _____

3. How did Raymond feel about the rights of African-Americans?

   _____

4. How did Rosa feel about her job?

   _____

5. What qualities would Rosa have to show to fight racism?

   _____

# Word Study

Use with student text page 298.

## Analyze the Suffix -ment

A **suffix** is a group of letters added to the end of a word. A suffix can change the meaning of the word.

The suffix *-ment* means "the act or state of." When the suffix *-ment* is added to a verb, the new word becomes a noun. If you add the suffix *-ment* to the verb *agree,* you form the noun *agreement* ("the act of agreeing").

**A.** ➤ Fill in the chart. Add *-ment* to each verb and write the new word's meaning.

| Base Word | Add *-ment* | New Word (Noun) | Meaning of New Word |
|---|---|---|---|
| argue | drop *e* + *-ment* | argument | |
| improve | + *-ment* | | |
| arrange | + *-ment* | | |
| move | + *-ment* | | |
| treat | + *-ment* | | |

**B.** ➤ Complete the sentences. Use the nouns in the chart.

1. Janil picked flowers and created a beautiful ____*arrangement*____.

2. Dance is a way to express feelings and ideas with _____.

3. Jackson showed great _____ in his guitar playing.

4. Angela is very kind. Her friends admire her _____ of others.

5. Roberto and Silvio were not speaking to each other. They got into an

_____.

# Grammar Focus

Use with student text page 298.

## Study Regular and Irregular Past Tense Verbs

A **past tense verb** describes an action that happened at a specific time in the past.

A **regular past tense** verb ends in *-ed*. For most regular verbs, add *-ed* to the verb. For example:

I walk**ed** home from school this afternoon.

An **irregular past tense verb** does not end in *-ed*. Irregular verbs form the past tense in different ways. For example:

I <u>ran</u> home from school this afternoon. (*Ran* is the past form of *run*.)

Look at these examples of regular and irregular past tense verbs:

| Simple Form of Regular Verbs | Regular Past Tense Verbs | Simple Form of Irregular Verbs | Irregular Past Tense Verbs |
|---|---|---|---|
| work | worked | wear | wore |
| stay | stayed | do | did |
| talk | talked | have | had |
| jump | jumped | choose | chose |

**A.** ➤ Rewrite the sentences by writing the verbs in past tense.

**Present Tense Sentence**

1. We <u>stay</u> at our friend's house.
2. She <u>talks</u> about her love of reading.
3. I <u>choose</u> the red notebook.
4. They <u>work</u> together at the school.
5. She <u>does</u> many things well.
6. He <u>wears</u> a red shirt and jeans.

**Past Tense Sentence**

1. _____ *We stayed at our friend's house.* _____
2. _____
3. _____
4. _____
5. _____
6. _____

**B.** ➤ Match the underlined word in the first column with its past tense form in the second column.

1. Sasha <u>walks</u> two miles a day. _____

2. I <u>understand</u> my math lesson. _____

3. The Oak Wood Tigers <u>win</u> more than any team.

   _____

4. The babies <u>play</u> with blocks. _____

5. Peter <u>keeps</u> a dream journal by his bed. _____

**played**

**kept**

**walked**

**understood**

# Grammar Focus

Use with student text page 298.

## Study Spelling Changes for Regular Past Tense Verbs

Sometimes the spelling of a verb changes when *-ed* is added to make it past tense. Look at some of these rules to learn how the spelling may change:

- Usually, if the verb ends in *-e*, just add *-d*. (*move—moved*).
- If a verb ends in a consonant plus *-y*, change the *y* to *i* and add *-ed*. (*cry—cried*).
- If a verb has one syllable, and the last two letters are a vowel + a consonant, the consonant is often doubled before adding *-ed*. (*hug—hugged*).

| Regular Verbs with Spelling Changes ||
|---|---|
| **Simple Form of Regular Verb** | **Past Form of Regular Verb** |
| live | liv**ed** |
| study | stud**ied** |
| stop | stop**ped** |

➤ Rewrite the sentences by writing the verbs in the past tense.

**Present Tense Sentence**

1. The trucks <u>carry</u> bales of hay.

2. Molly and Dan <u>shop</u> in a bakery.

3. The dancers <u>move</u> to the music.

4. The clowns in the circus <u>juggle</u> oranges.

5. Jana and Shane <u>cry</u> during a sad movie.

6. The cars <u>slip</u> on the icy roads.

**Past Tense Sentence**

1. _____ *The trucks carried bales of hay.* _____

2. _____
   _____

3. _____
   _____

4. _____
   _____

5. _____
   _____

6. _____
   _____

Student
Handbook

# From Reading to Writing

*Use with student text page 299.*

## Prewrite for a Biography

Suppose you are going to write a biography about someone you know well. Write some notes below. Put them in chronological order (the order in which events happened). Include all the important facts you can think of.

_____

_____

_____

_____

_____

_____

➤ Use the checklist to make sure you included all of the most important information about this person.

**Prewriting Checklist for a Biography**

Title of biography: _____

**What I did:**

_____ 1. I included their name and when and where they were born.

_____ 2. I wrote down some important events in his or her life.

_____ 3. I put the events in chronological order.

_____ 4. I included information about what the person likes to do or how he or she feels about something.

_____ 5. I thought about how I might describe this person.

_____ 6. I included how I know this person.

VISIONS Unit 5 • Chapter 1 Rosa Parks

## Across Content Areas

*Use with student text page 299.*

### Learn About Constitutional Amendments

**What is the U.S. Constitution?**

People in the United States have rights and freedoms that are protected by writings, or *documents*. One very important document is the U.S. Constitution. Our government is based upon this document.

**How has the U.S. Constitution changed since it was first written?**

The U.S. Constitution was written for the purpose of protecting the rights and freedoms of every person in the nation. However, it has not stayed exactly the same over the years. There have been additions to the U.S. Constitution. These changes are called amendments.

**What is the purpose of the amendments?**

There are more than 20 amendments to the U.S. Constitution. Many of them add protection for each person's rights and freedoms.

| Some of the Amendments to the U.S. Constitution | | |
|---|---|---|
| **Amendment** | **Rights and Freedoms** | **Examples** |
| The First Amendment | Americans can say and write what they want. | The editor of a newspaper writes an article to express his opinion about the playgrounds in city parks. |
| The Thirteenth Amendment | There is to be no slavery in the United States. | Slavery ended in all American states in 1865. |
| The Nineteenth Amendment | Women who are 18 years old are allowed to vote. | Female college students who are United States citizens . . . can vote. |

➤ Write Notes

Imagine that you want to share your opinion about something that needs to change in your town or state. Write notes about what you want to see changed and why.

**Notes**

_____

_____

_____

_____

# Build Vocabulary

*Use with student text page 301.*

## Identify Antonyms and Related Words

Words that have opposite meanings are antonyms. For example, *cold* is an antonym for the word *hot*.

➤ Read the words and the definitions. Then read the sentences and write the antonym for each underlined word.

**Word and Definition**

**brave** unafraid of danger
**decorated** made something beautiful
**detract** take something good away from something
**fitting** suitable, proper
**pleased** happy, satisfied
**stressed** express something strongly
**undivided** together, whole

### Word in a Sentence

1. It was <u>fitting</u> for President Lincoln to give a speech at Gettysburg. _____

2. The teachers <u>decorated</u> the school gym with balloons. _____

3. If you let an old baseball card get wet, you may <u>detract</u> from its value. _____

4. My school teacher always <u>stressed</u> the importance of spelling. _____

5. Statues are often built to honor <u>brave</u> soldiers who fought for their country. _____

6. The students were <u>undivided</u> in their opinion that there should be a longer lunch hour. _____

7. When the work was finished, the townspeople were very <u>pleased</u>. _____

### Antonym

a. add
b. ignored
c. improper
d. disappointed
e. afraid
f. split
g. simplified

# Writing: Punctuation

*Use with student text page 312.*

## Use Quotation Marks

Quotation marks ("...") are placed before and after the exact words that a character says. There is a comma either at the beginning or the end of most quotations.

**Correct:** The teacher said, "Who would like to go on a class trip?"
**Incorrect:** The teacher said, Who would like to go on a class trip?

The quotation marks help the reader to understand what the teacher said. The words people say can also be noted first in a sentence.

"Let's plan the class trip," said Mrs. Greenway.

Read these sentences from "The Gettysburg Address." Notice the way quotation marks are used to show someone is speaking.

"My speech does not express how deeply I feel about these men," he thought. "It is what I would call a short, short speech," he said.

**A.** ➤ Edit these sentences. Write *yes* if a sentence needs quotation marks. Write the quotation marks in the correct places. If a sentence does not need quotation marks, write *no*.

1. ____*yes*____ Lincoln said, "I must write a better speech for these men."

2. _____ Mr. Wills asked important people to speak at Gettysburg.

3. _____ Edward Everett planned to give a long speech.

4. _____ Lincoln thought, I will make my speech short.

5. _____ Mr. Everett spoke for nearly two hours.

6. _____ We will sing a special song, said the choir leader.

7. _____ The president spoke for a short time.

8. _____ One of the people in the crowd shouted, That was the best speech I have heard in many years!

**B.** ➤ Edit the paragraph. Write the missing quotation marks.

Although President Lincoln was busy thinking about the Civil War, he still knew it was important for him to travel to Gettysburg. He said, I have to honor the brave soldiers who gave their lives. He knew Mr. Everett would be speaking. I don't want to speak for a long time, said President Lincoln.

# Elements of Literature

Use with student text page 313.

## Identify Words for Their Effect

Writers of speeches want their words to have an effect on the listeners. They choose words that will express a certain message or mood (feeling).

Read these words from "The Gettysburg Address." They show the message and feeling that President Lincoln wanted to express in his speech.

"I want people everywhere to understand what freedom means to us and how much we owe to the brave soldiers who died at Gettysburg."

**A.** ➤ Read the words from Lincoln's speech. Choose the sentence that tells the message Lincoln expressed.

1. . . . dedicated to the proposition that <u>all men are created equal</u>
   **a.** All people should be treated the same.
   **b.** All people should have the same amount of money.

2. We have come to dedicate a portion of that field. . . . It is altogether fitting and proper that we should do this.
   **a.** The battlefield was the right size.
   **b.** It was right to dedicate the battlefield.

3. The brave men [the soldiers], living and dead, who struggled here, have consecrated it.
   **a.** The soldiers were hard workers.
   **b.** The soldiers were great men who deserve honor (respect).

**B.** ➤ Think about Lincoln's speech. If possible, listen to the audio recording. Then write whether you think these statements are true or false.

1. Lincoln only cared about winning the war. He did not care about people from the South. ___*false*___

2. Lincoln cared deeply about the soldiers who died. _____

3. Lincoln felt that the soldiers died for an unimportant cause. _____

4. Lincoln felt that the soldiers cared about their nation. _____

5. Lincoln felt that the American government should be run by the people of the nation. _____

# Word Study

Use with student text page 314.

## Use the Suffixes -or and -er

You can add the suffix -or to some verbs to make them nouns. The noun means "someone who does something."

sail + -or = sail**or** (a person who sails)

If the verb ends in e, you must drop the e before you add -or. For example:

creat~~e~~ + -or = creat**or** (a person who creates)

Other verbs take the suffix -er to make them nouns that show someone who does something. For example:

sing + -er = sing**er** (a person who sings)

Here, too, if a word ends in e, you drop the e before you add -er. For example:

settl~~e~~ + -er → settl**er** (a person who settles)

**A.** ➤ Fill in the chart. Form nouns by adding -or to each verb.

| Verb | + -or | New Word | Meaning of New Word |
|------|-------|----------|---------------------|
| act | + -or | | |
| translate | drop e + -or | | |
| narrate | drop e + -or | | |

**B.** ➤ Change each verb in the box to a noun ending in -er. Then complete each sentence with the correct new word.

| Verb |
|------|
| paint |
| buy |
| write |

**1.** Abraham Lincoln was a good _____ of speeches.

**2.** They have not sold their house yet because they cannot find a _____.

**3.** They hired a _____ to create a mural for their wall.

# Grammar Focus

*Use with student text page 314.*

### Identify Phrases with Verb + Object + Infinitive

A **phrase** is a group of words that are part of a sentence. Some phrases have a *verb*, an *object*, and an *infinitive*.

|  | **Verb** | **Object** | **Infinitive** |  |
|---|---|---|---|---|
| Janice | wants | Maurice | to join | her club. |

In the sentence, *wants* is the verb. *Maurice* is the object. The object receives the action of the verb. The infinitive is the word *to* and the verb *join*.

|  | **Verb** | **Object** | **Infinitive** |  |
|---|---|---|---|---|
| The politician | asked | people | to vote | for him. |

In this sentence, *asked* is the verb. The word *people* is the object. The infinitive is the word *to* and the verb *vote*.

➤ Fill in the chart. Write the verb, the object, and the infinitive for each underlined phrase.

1. My aunt Mary <u>expects me to visit</u> her on Friday.
2. Hari <u>needed James to hold</u> the ladder.
3. Sally often <u>asks Martina to drive</u> her home from school.
4. The driving test <u>requires students to learn</u> about stop signs.
5. The bandleader <u>tells drummers to count</u> carefully.
6. Ira's grandfather <u>allows him to use</u> his computer.

| Verb | Object | Infinitive |
|---|---|---|
| 1. expects | me | to visit |
| 2. | | |
| 3. | | |
| 4. | | |
| 5. | | |
| 6. | | |

## Grammar Focus

*Use with student text page 314.*

### Identify Direct Objects

A direct object receives the action of the verb. The direct object answers the questions *whom* or *what*.

     **Verb   Direct Object**
The goalie <u>blocked</u>  <u>the kick</u>.

What did the goalie block? He blocked *the kick*.

**A.** ➤ Underline the verb and the direct object in each sentence. Label the verb with *V* and the direct object with *D.O.* The first one has been done for you.

       *V*   *D.O.*
1. Simon will <u>meet</u> his <u>mother</u> at the shopping mall.

2. Mrs. Hanover found a sweater she likes.

3. They bought some gifts for their cousins.

4. Simon thanked his uncle for his new CD.

5. We saw lions and tigers at the zoo.

**B.** ➤ Complete these sentences with direct objects.

1. The kids bought _____ for lunch.

2. My grandmother cooks _____ very well.

3. Susana gave me _____ for my birthday.

4. We like _____ for breakfast.

5. If you are sick, see _____.

Student
Handbook

Name _____ Date _____

# From Reading to Writing

*Use with student text page 315.*

**Prepare for Writing a Speech**

Imagine that you are running for class president. You are writing a speech to persuade your classmates to vote for you. Answer the questions to help you write a draft. On the lines below, write a paragraph that could be part of a first draft. (You may make up some of the details.)

1. What qualities do you have that would help you be a good president?

_____

_____

2. What have you done that shows you are a responsible person?

_____

_____

3. What ideas do you have for raising money for your class?

_____

_____

4. What are some words you can use that will convince people to vote for you?

_____

_____

5. What examples can you give that show you are good at working with others?

_____

_____

**Paragraph for a First Draft**

_____

_____

_____

_____

_____

_____

_____

_____

## Across Content Areas

Use with student text page 315.

### Use Math Vocabulary

Some words show amount. For example, the first words of the Gettysburg Address are, "Four score and seven years ago." Because the word *score* stands for 20 years, you can figure out the number of years that Lincoln was talking about:

| **Four** | | **score** | | |
|---|---|---|---|---|
| 4 | × | 20 | = | 80 |

**and seven years** = 7
_____
87 years

Look at the charts below to find other words and the amounts they show.

| Words That Show Amounts | |
|---|---|
| **Word** | **Amount** |
| 1 hour | 60 minutes |
| 1 week | 7 days |
| 1 year | 12 months |

| Words That Show Amounts | |
|---|---|
| **Word** | **Amount** |
| 1 decade | 10 years |
| 1 century | 100 years |

### Solve Problems

➤ Answer the questions. Use the chart. The first one has been done for you.

1. Imagine that it is the year 2004. A certain town was founded three centuries ago. In what year was it founded?

   *In 1704 (One century is 100 years. Three centuries ago would be 300 years before 2004.)*

2. Eva's music lesson is 30 minutes long. What part of an hour is her music lesson?

   _____

3. Mr. Gomez asked students to write a report that was due in two weeks. In how many days is the paper due?

   _____

4. There is a presidential election every four years. How many presidential elections will there be in one decade?

   _____

5. Marco's baby sister is 17 months old. Is she younger or older than one year old? By how many months?

   _____

# Build Vocabulary

*Use with student text page 317.*

## Understand Words in Context

**Context** is the words and sentences that surround a specific word. The context often helps give you an idea of what a new word might mean.

Amil felt tired. He was <u>weary</u> from carrying his backpack home.
The context in these sentences tell you that *weary* means *tired*.

**A.** ➤ Match the underlined word in each sentence to its definition. Use context to help you.

**Word in a Sentence**

1. ___*e*___   Wanda expressed her <u>gratitude</u> to her parents for the new computer.

2. _____   The weather was so cold and dry that my hands got <u>chapped</u>.

3. _____   In baseball, a ball that gets hit outside the <u>boundary</u> of the field is a foul ball.

4. _____   Before the settlers came to the land, they said <u>farewell</u> to the friends they left behind.

5. _____   The fish jumped into the air and was once again <u>submerged</u> in the sea.

6. _____   After swimming several laps in the swimming pool, Cassandra climbed out, <u>exhausted</u>.

**Definition**

**a.** goodbye

**b.** dividing line

**c.** very tired

**d.** dried, cracked

**e.** thankfulness

**f.** underwater

**B.** ➤ Underline the adjective in each sentence. Place two underlines under the noun it describes.

1. The <u>bare</u> <u>trees</u> showed that winter had arrived.

2. We woke up and saw falling snow outside.

3. My sisters and I grabbed our red sleds.

# Writing: Spelling

Use with student text page 326.

## Spell Regular Plurals

When you make a word plural (showing more than one), you usually add -s to the word. Some words do not follow this rule, but most words do.

Read this sentence from "So Far from the Bamboo Grove," and notice the underlined plural words:

> He wanted to tell Mrs. Kim many <u>things</u> to express his gratitude, but the <u>tears</u> came and his chest tightened.

**A.** ➤ Complete the sentences. Use the plural form of the word before each sentence.

1. <hip> Mrs. Kim put the rucksack in a burlap bag tied with a long rope and told

   him to carry it around his _____*hips*_____ like a Korean.

2. <soldier> American _____ controlled southern Korea.

3. <time> Just before they vanished into the deep forest he waved a towel three
   _____ for a final farewell.

4. <friend> At their doorway his _____ waved back.

5. <Communist> The river was well guarded by the _____.

6. <eye> He cast his _____ onto the dark, wide river and wondered if
   he could swim across.

7. <direction> Gunfire burst in the air, echoing in a thousand _____.

8. <bullet> He could hear the _____ piercing the waters all around him.

**B.** ➤ Find the word in each sentence that should be plural. Write the plural form on the lines.

1. When it gets really cold outside, Gale puts on her blue glove. _____*gloves*_____

2. She likes to go outside with two of her best friend. _____

3. They will often make a pile of snowball and throw them at the trees.

   _____

4. Then the three girl went inside and made some hot chocolate. _____

5. Sometimes, they will bake a lot of cookie to eat. _____

6. They make enough snack to share with Gale's twin brother. _____

○ # Elements of Literature

*Use with student text page 327.*

## Use Text to Analyze Motivation

**Motivation** is the reason why a character does something. Sometimes, the author directly tells us a character's motivation.

Juana bought her coach a gift to thank her.

Other times, the author provides text clues for the reader to figure out a character's motivation.

After Juana thought about all the ways her coach had helped her, she bought her a gift.

**A.** ➤ Answer the questions below each sentence. Use the clues in the text to figure out the characters' motivation.

Mrs. Kim packed large rice balls in a bamboo box and Mr. Kim handed Hideyo a little money. Hideyo tried to refuse the money, for Mr. Kim was a poor farmer . . . but Mr. Kim insisted.

**1.** Why does Mr. Kim behave the way he does?

*He is a generous person who cares about Hideyo.*

○ **2.** Why does Hideyo behave the way he does?

_____

Hideyo wanted to tell Mrs. Kim many things to express his gratitude, but the tears came and his chest tightened. Mrs. Kim held his hands and cried, *"Aigo!"* an expression of sadness.

**3.** Why can't Hideyo tell his feelings to Mrs. Kim?

_____

**4.** What feeling does Mrs. Kim show Hideyo?

_____

Again gunfire. . . . When Hideyo finally reached the south side he lay as dead when the light shone his way, then crawled toward the bushes, exhausted.
He had escaped across the dangerous thirty-eighth parallel. He took a deep breath of freedom.

**5.** What makes Hideyo travel until he is so tired he can hardly move?

_____

○ **6.** Why does Hideyo take a deep breath?

_____

VISIONS C Activity Book • Copyright © Heinle

# Word Study

Use with student text page 328.

## Identify Root Words

Many English words come from other languages. The words they come from are called **root words**. Some dictionaries tell where the word came from. This is the word's **origin.**

> **dismiss** /dis mis´/ *verb* to send away: *The teacher dismissed the students at the end of class.* [Latin *mittere* to send]

— Word Origin

Read the root words and their meanings. Then look at the words that can be made from the root words.

| Root Word | Root Word Meaning | English Word | English Word Meaning |
|-----------|-------------------|--------------|----------------------|
| *mittere* | to send | dis*miss* | to send away |
| *movere* | to move | *mot*ion | movement |
| *vertere* | to turn | re*verse* | to turn around |
| *videre* | to see | *vis*ion | ability to see |

**A.** ➤ Complete the sentences. Use the words in the chart.

1. The bell rang, but the teacher waited a few minutes to _____ the class.

2. Frank needs eyeglasses to improve his _____.

3. The water was going down the sink drain with the _____ of a circle.

4. To get out of a parking space, back up the car and drive it in _____.

**B.** ➤ Write a sentence for each new word in the chart.

1. _____

2. _____

3. _____

4. _____

# Grammar Focus

*Use with student text page 328.*

### Use the Conjunction *So That*

A **clause** is a group of words that has a subject and a verb. A **conjunction** connects clauses in a sentence.

In the examples below, the clauses are underlined. The conjunctions have two underlines.

Warren went to the store, <u>but</u> he came home early.

Samantha took the train, <u>and</u> she bought her ticket before she left.

The conjunction *so that* is used to give a reason.

I ate a big breakfast <u>so that</u> I wouldn't get hungry on the hike.

➤ **Match** the clauses to make sentences. Write the sentences below.

| | |
|---|---|
| He wore dark clothes | so that he wouldn't get lost. |
| Mrs. Kim gave him some food | so that the soldiers wouldn't see him at night. |
| He moved silently | so that no one would hear him. |
| His friends gave him a map | so that he wouldn't be hungry. |
| Mrs. Kim put the rucksack in a bag | so that Hideyo would look like a Korean. |

1. _____

2. _____

3. _____

4. _____

5. _____

## Grammar Focus

Use with student text page 328.

### Understand Dependent Clauses

A complex sentence contains an independent clause and one or more **dependent clauses.**

An independent clause can stand alone as a sentence. A dependent clause has a subject and a verb, but is not a complete sentence. It cannot stand alone.

**independent clause**        **dependent clause**

Irene needed a haircut because her hair was getting too long.

Here is a list of conjunctions that are often used to start dependent clauses: *after, although, because, before, if, since, unless, until,* and *while.*

**A.** ➤ Underline the dependent clause in each sentence. Circle the conjunction.

1. My dog, Toby, will not eat his dinner (until) I come home from school.

2. He stands by the door waiting until my family comes into the house.

3. Toby is used to being home alone because he has been many times before.

4. He usually naps while I am at school.

5. Sometimes he jumps up if he hears the mail carrier.

6. He will sit at the window after the mail carrier walks away.

**B.** ➤ Write sentences with the conjunctions that are given.

1. after _____

2. because _____

3. if _____

4. before _____

5. so that _____

Student
Handbook

# From Reading to Writing

Use with student text page 329.

### Edit Historical Fiction

➤ Use the checklist to make sure you included all of the most important information that should go into a work of historical fiction.

**Checklist for Historical Fiction**

Name of story: _____

**What I did:**

_____ **1.** I chose a real time and place for my story.

_____ **2.** I wrote what happened to my character.

_____ **3.** I told about my character's motivation.

_____ **4.** I put the events in chronological order.

_____ **5.** I wrote a title for my story.

_____ **6.** I indented my paragraphs.

## Across Content Areas

Use with student text page 329.

### Use Punctuation and Intonation

In "So Far from the Bamboo Grove," Hideyo meets Hee Cho as Hideyo is trying to escape from Korea. At the end of the conversation, Hee Cho says to Hideyo:

*Chigŭm kaseyo* (Go now)!

Notice the exclamation point. It adds feeling to the statement, showing that there is danger and that Hideyo should hurry so he will not be caught.

An exclamation point shows force and emotion. A question mark shows that an answer is needed.

➤ Read the sentences below. Notice how the exclamation point and the question mark help tell the reader what *intonation*, or tone of voice, to use.

| Punctuation and Intonation | | |
|---|---|---|
| **Sentence with Exclamation Point or Question Mark** | **Intonation** | |
| I can't believe it! I won the election! | These sentences show excitement. | 🙂 |
| When will you arrive? | This sentence shows someone is looking for information. | 😲 |
| Turn the light on! I'm scared! | These sentences show fear. | 😱 |
| Should we try to call them? | This sentence shows that someone wants advice. | 😕 |

### Write an Advertisement

Imagine that you are creating an advertisement for a new product—a toy, a food item, an electronic gadget—anything you wish. Write four sentences that will make your reader interested in the product. Make two of the sentences questions. Make the other two sentences end in an exclamation point.

_____

_____

_____

_____

_____

# Build Vocabulary

*Use with student text page 331.*

## Use Words in Sentences

**Use Words in Sentences**

When you read the definition of a word, you will understand it better if it is used in a sentence.

Look at the words in the chart. Then read the definitions and sentences to understand each word better.

| Word | Definition | Sentence |
|------|-----------|----------|
| disabilities | things that take away a normal ability | The blind man's *disabilities* led him to listen to books on audiocassettes. |
| refuge | a place of safety | The kitten was out in the cold rain, looking for a *refuge* from the storm. |
| illusion | a mistaken idea | He thought he had discovered gold, but the rocks were an *illusion*. |
| critiquing | evaluating someone's work | The judges are *critiquing* each skater's performance. |
| obscure | hard to see or understand | My teacher explained the process, but I found the information *obscure*. |
| afloat | surviving (connotative meaning) | Graham has been struggling to learn geometry, but he is staying *afloat*. |

➤ Write a sentence for each word in the chart.

1. _____

2. _____

3. _____

4. _____

5. _____

6. _____

# Writing: Punctuation

*Use with student text page 338.*

## Punctuate by Using Periods

Periods are used in two ways. First, they mark the end of most statements. They are also used in **abbreviations** (shortened words).

My mother asked Mrs. Williams if she would work with me.

Note the period after *Mrs.* in the sentence above. *Mrs.* is a title that some married women use. Other common abbreviations are *Mr.* (a title for men), *Ms.* (a title for any woman), and *Dr.* (doctor).

**A.** ➤ Edit the paragraph. Add the missing periods.

Samantha had been having a difficult time in school She did not do well in most subjects However, she enjoyed her creative writing class There she was allowed to write in whatever way she wanted It was a chance for her to feel successful Once people realized she was learning disabled, her teachers could help her learn in a better way She still writes today and teaches others about what it is like to be learning disabled

**B.** ➤ Edit the paragraph. Add the missing periods.

I tried to work on my math lesson, but I felt really sick. I asked my teacher, Ms Lopez, if I could see the nurse. "Of course," Ms. Lopez said. I then went to visit Mr Clark, the school nurse. He examined me and told me that I had a fever. He called my mother and said that she should take me to our family's doctor. My mother answered, "Thank you for calling, Mr Clark. I will make an appointment with Dr Jackson right away."

# Elements of Literature

*Use with student text page 339.*

## Recognize Figurative Language

Writers often describe one thing by comparing it to another thing. This is called **figurative language**. "Alone" and "Samantha's Story" both use figurative language. Figurative language helps the reader form pictures in his or her mind. These pictures help readers better understand the text.

A place where the sun and its flowers bow in shadow

The sun does not really bow. Flowers bend, but they do not bow like people. The writer uses these words to make the sun and the flowers seem gentle.

**A.** ➤ Each sentence includes figurative language. Describe the pictures you form in your mind from each sentence.

1. The tree stood gracefully in the moonlight.

_____

2. The talented singer shone like a star as she performed.

_____

3. The plane flew above a sea of clouds.

_____

4. The basketball player flew to the net with the ball.

_____

**B.** ➤ Choose one of the sentences above. Draw the picture you form in your mind from the figurative language in the sentence.

| Picture in My Mind |
| --- |
|  |

# Word Study

Use with student text page 340.

## Use Word Parts to Understand Meaning

Many words come from **root words.** If you know the meaning of the root word, you can often figure out what the new word means.

The word *light* can mean "brightness." It can also be a verb meaning "to add brightness." Some words come from *light* and have related meanings.

**A.** ➤ Fill in the chart. The first one has been done for you.

| Root Word | Add to the Word | New Word | Meaning of New Word |
|---|---|---|---|
| light | 1. *sun-* + light | sunlight | 1. light that comes from the sun |
| | 2. *moon-* + light | | 2. light that comes from the moon |
| | 3. *de-* + light + *-ful* | | 3. full of a light, joyful feeling |
| | 4. light + *-ly* | | 4. not heavily or seriously |
| | 5. light + *-er* | | 5. with more light |
| | 6. *en-* + light + *-en* | | 6. educate (add more "light" to a subject) |

**B.** ➤ Complete the sentences. Use the words you wrote in the chart. The first one has been done for you.

1. During the summer, the _____*sunlight*_____ lasts until almost nine o'clock.

2. Vera and Roberto went to a lecture that would _____ them about the stars and the planets.

3. The dance performance of the kindergarten class was not perfect, but the children's smiling faces were _____ to see.

4. Last night, the sky was very dark. There was no _____ anywhere.

5. The sun bleached the fabric of the couch near the window, so the color is much _____ than before.

6. The ballet dancer stepped _____ across the stage floor.

# Grammar Focus

Use with student text page 340.

## Use Regular Superlative Adjectives

**Superlative adjectives** compare three or more things. Superlative adjectives indicate the most of a quality. For example, the superlative *youngest,* means the "most young."

Many superlative adjectives end in *-est.* Here are some examples of how adjectives change to the superlative form:

| Adjective | Superlative Adjective |
|-----------|----------------------|
| tall | tall**est** |
| heavy | heav**iest** |

The words in the first column become superlative adjectives by adding *-est.* If the word ends in *-e,* add *-st.* If the word ends in a consonant plus *y,* change the *y* to *i* and then add *-est.*

**A.** ➤ Fill in the chart. Change each adjective to a superlative adjective. The first one has been done for you.

| Regular Superlative Adjectives ||
|-----------------|----------------------|
| **Adjectives** | **Superlative Adjectives** |
| **1.** nice | nicest |
| **2.** bright | |
| **3.** fine | |
| **4.** sunny | |
| **5.** clear | |
| **6.** large | |
| **7.** young | |
| **8.** friendly | |

**B.** ➤ Complete the sentences by using the superlative form of each adjective in parentheses.

1. Mr. Teller had the (bright) _____ flowers of all the people in his neighborhood.

2. It is the (clear) _____ sky we have had in a long time.

3. The (sunny) _____ day was on Saturday.

4. Jennifer is the (young) _____ child in her family.

5. Mrs. Jones is the (friendly) _____ person on the block.

Name _____  Date _____

## Grammar Focus

*Use with student text page 341.*

### Understand Regular Comparative Adjectives

Adjectives that end in *-er* are called **comparative adjectives.** They compare two things. For example, *old* becomes *older*.

Mom has an <u>old</u> car, but Dad has an <u>older</u> car.

If an adjective ends in *e*, drop the *e* and then add *-er* to form the comparative adjective. For example, *simple* becomes *simpler*.

If an adjective ends in *y,* change the *y* to *i* and then add *-er* to form the comparative adjective. For example, *funny* becomes *funnier*.

**A.** ➤ Fill in the chart. Change each adjective to a comparative adjective. The first one has been done for you.

**B.** ➤ Write a sentence for each adjective below. Use the adjective, its comparative form, and its superlative.

1. fast

    *Kayla is fast, but Marco is faster. Ava is*

    *the fastest.*

2. clean

    _____

    _____

3. sleepy

    _____

4. long

    _____

5. late

    _____

6. quiet

    _____

| Regular Comparative Adjectives | |
| Adjectives | Comparative Adjectives |
| --- | --- |
| **1.** nice | nicer |
| **2.** clear | |
| **3.** sleepy | |
| **4.** clean | |
| **5.** short | |
| **6.** long | |
| **7.** late | |
| **8.** quiet | |

Student Handbook

VISIONS  Unit 5 • Chapter 4  *Alone and Samantha's Story*

VISIONS C  Activity Book • Copyright © Heinle

Name _____   Date _____

# From Reading to Writing

*Use with student text page 341.*

## Prewrite for a Poem

Think about a place that is special to you—it can be a room in your house, a place you like to visit, a place that interests you, or a place that you think is fun.

**A.** ➤ Brainstorm ideas and fill in the word web. Write the name of your special place in the middle oval. In the other ovals, write words that describe your place.

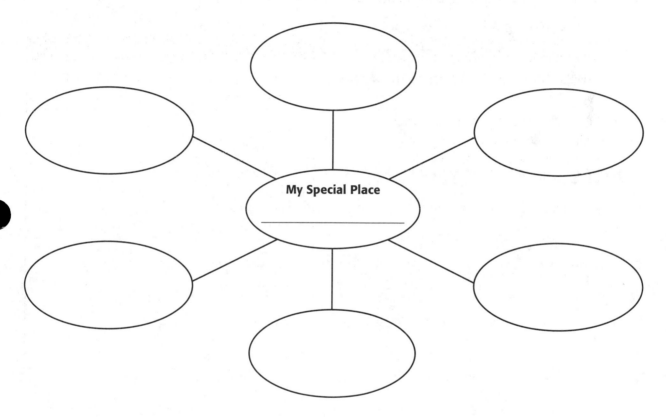

My Special Place

_____

**B.** ➤ Write four lines of your poem. Use your word web to help you.

_____

_____

_____

_____

## Across Content Areas

Use with student text page 341.

### Learn About Genres

A **genre** is a type of writing. There are many different genres. Read the list which shows a few different genres.

**Fiction:** stories that include made-up characters and events

**Poetry:** writing that is usually arranged in groups of lines called *stanzas* and includes words that help readers form pictures in their minds

**Drama:** writing that is designed to be performed on stage

**Fable:** writing that may have animals as the main characters

**Biography:** writing that tells the story of a real person's life

**Autobiography:** the story of the author's life

### Match the Genres

➤ Match each description with one of the genres listed in the book.

1. A book that the author writes about her early childhood

_____

2. A book about a young man who searches for a hidden treasure map

_____

3. A play that includes dialogue for actors to say out loud

_____

4. A book that describes the real-life events of a U.S. president

_____

5. A story about a turtle who wins a big race

_____

6. A piece of writing that uses rhyming words like *find* and *mind*

_____

# Build Vocabulary

*Use with student text page 351.*

## Define Words

➤ Rewrite the sentences by replacing each underlined word with a word from the box. The first one has been done for you.

---

**Word and Definition**

**extravagant**  using or spending too much
**festive**  joyful
**convenient**  acceptable; fitting one's needs
**reform**  change for the better
**furnish**  give or supply
**benevolence**  goodness
**meager**  very little
**apprentice**  a person learning a skill from an expert

---

1. Her fancy clothes are <u>wasteful</u>.

   *Her fancy clothes are extravagant.*

2. The carpenter is showing his <u>assistant</u> how to build a wooden table.

   _____

3. People try to <u>change</u> laws that are unfair.

   _____

4. My mother likes to <u>supply</u> hot chocolate after we play in the snow.

   _____

5. The circus always has a <u>happy</u> group of clowns and jugglers.

   _____

6. I tried hard, but I could save only a <u>small</u> amount of money.

   _____

7. Mark shows his <u>kindness</u> by feeding stray cats.

   _____

8. We will find a time to meet that is <u>suitable</u> for both of us.

   _____

# Writing: Punctuation

Use with student text page 360.

## Punctuate by Using Dashes

Use a **dash** to show a pause.

He ran to the store—then he ran home.

➤ Rewrite the sentences by including dashes. The first one has been done for you.

1. Cratchit why are you using coal at this time of day?

   *Cratchit why are you using coal at this time of day?* _____

2. But, sir I cannot write well when my fingers are so cold.

   _____

3. Merry Christmas, uncle you look just as pleased as usual.

   _____

4. We would like you to come for dinner that is all I came to ask.

   _____

5. We would like to ask you to make a donation just a small amount.

   _____

6. You have to be joking do you think I just give money away?

   _____

# Elements of Literature

Use with student text page 361.

## Understand Mood in Stage Directions

**Stage directions** tell what the characters are supposed to do. They are often in parentheses (. . .) and *italics*.

Fred (*Cheerfully*): A Merry Christmas, uncle!
Scrooge (*Without looking up*): Bah! Humbug!

Stage directions also show the mood of a play. These stage directions show that Fred is happy and that Scrooge is not happy

➤ Read the stage directions. Underline the mood or condition the directions communicate to the reader. The first one has been done for you.

1. Bob (*Going back to stool*): Yes, sir. (*Rubs hands over candle. Huddles in muffler.*)
   **a.** Bob is very cold.
   **b.** Bob is very warm.

2. Scrooge (*Glaring at BOB*): *You'll* want all day tomorrow, I suppose?
   **a.** Scrooge is happy that Bob wants to take time off of work.
   **b.** Scrooge is angry that Bob wants to take time off of work.

3. Scrooge (*banging down ruler*): Bah! Humbug!
   **a.** Scrooge is angry.
   **b.** Scrooge is happy.

4. Fred: I have always thought of Christmas-time as a good time . . . (*BOB claps his hands, then, embarrassed at his impulse, huddles over his work.*)
   **a.** Bob is embarrassed about his action and afraid that Scrooge will be angry.
   **b.** Bob wants everyone to know he agrees with Fred.

5. Solicitor: *Good afternoon!* (*SOLICITOR goes out, shaking his head.*)
   **a.** The solicitor is offended.
   **b.** The solicitor is cheerful.

# Word Study

Use with student text page 362.

## Analyze Contractions

**Contractions** are used to make words shorter. They are formed by joining two words together. Letters are dropped and replaced by an apostrophe (').

do + not → don't      I + am → I'm
can + not → can't     he + will → he'll
were + not → weren't   she + is → she's

**A.** ➤ Fill in the chart. Form contractions by combining the words in the first column. The first one has been done for you.

| Subject and Verb | Contraction |
|---|---|
| **1.** I could not | I couldn't |
| **2.** I did not | |
| **3.** he is not | |
| **4.** we will | |
| **5.** he will | |
| **6.** I am | |
| **7.** she is | |
| **8.** they are | |

**B.** ➤ Rewrite each underlined word as a contraction.

1. <u>I am</u> sorry that I have not written for such a long time.

_____

2. <u>I will</u> tell you about my new musical activities.

_____

3. I <u>did not</u> think I would be interested in joining the school chorus.

_____

4. I <u>was not</u> a very good singer.

_____

5. Mr. DeGeneris says <u>he is</u> going to be the new music teacher.

_____

# Grammar Focus

Use with student text page 362.

## Use the Present Perfect Tense

The **present perfect tense** often describes actions or conditions that started in the past and continue to the present.

Alicia <u>has lived</u> in Los Angeles for a year.

The present perfect verb *has lived* shows that Alicia lived in Los Angeles in the past, and she still lives there now.

| The Present Perfect Tense | | | |
|---|---|---|---|
| **Subject** | **Auxiliary Verb** | **Past Participle of Verb** | |
| I, You, We, They | have | lived | in Los Angeles for a year. |
| He, She | has | | |

Past participles can be regular or irregular. Add *-d* or *-ed* to the simple form of the verb for regular verbs. You must memorize the irregular verbs. Here are a few irregular verbs.

**Irregular Verbs**

| | | |
|---|---|---|
| be—gone | have—had | eat—eaten |
| go—gone | know—known | do—done |

**A.** ➤ Fill in the blanks with *has* or *have*.

1. Grandmother _____ been in her garden all day.

2. I _____ waited for you for an hour!

3. My brother and I _____ walked to school all year.

4. We _____ gone to this school since September.

5. Yuri _____ had this skateboard for just two days.

**B.** ➤ Fill in the blanks with the present perfect tense of the verb (*have* or *has* plus the past participle of the verb).

1. My mother _____ (work) at the clinic for three years.

2. Julia _____ (know) Germán all her life.

3. The kids _____ (eat) at that table every day for a month.

4. Marcia _____ (do) the dishes every night this week. Now it's your turn!

5. My brother and I _____ (walk) to school since September.

# Grammar Focus

Use with student text page 362.

## Use the Present Perfect Tense of Verbs with Questions, Negatives, and Contractions

To form the present perfect tense in questions, put the auxiliary verb before the subject.

       **subject**

<u>Have</u>  you  <u>walked</u> around the block?

To form the present perfect tense with a negative, the word *not* is placed after the auxiliary verb.

I <u>have</u> **not** <u>walked</u> around the block.

Here are the contractions for the present perfect tense.

| Subject + Auxiliary Verb | | Auxiliary Verb + *Not* | |
|---|---|---|---|
| **Full Form** | **Contracted Form** | **Full Form** | **Contracted Form** |
| I have<br>you have<br>we have<br>they have | I've<br>you've<br>we've<br>they've | have not | haven't |
| he has<br>she has<br>it has | he's<br>she's<br>it's | has not | hasn't |

➤ Rewrite the sentences into the form given.

1. They <u>have been</u> in the library for an hour.

    Question: _____ *Have they been in the library for an hour?* _____

2. I <u>have lived</u> here for two years.

    Negative: _____

3. John and Judi <u>have not eaten</u> at home all week.

    Contraction: _____

        4. You <u>have known</u> about the party for a week.

          Question: _____

Student Handbook

        5. They <u>have gone</u> to this school for a long time.

          Negative: _____

# From Reading to Writing

*Use with student text page 363.*

## Edit a Persuasive Letter

➤ Use the checklist to edit the persuasive letter you wrote in Chapter 1.

**Editing Checklist for a Persuasive Letter**

Title of the persuasive letter: _____

**What I did:**

_____ **1.** I organized my letter.

_____ **2.** I listed two reasons why Mr. Scrooge should give money
to needy people.

_____ **3.** I listed at least one reason why Mr. Scrooge might object
to giving money.

_____ **4.** I listed at least one way to respond to Mr. Scrooge's objection.

_____ **5.** I used the model in my textbook as a guide for my letter.

Name _____  Date _____

## Across Content Areas

*Use with student text page 363.*

### Use a Storyboard

**Storyboards** are used to show what characters, settings, and scenes will look like.

**A.** ➤ Fill in the storyboard. Use pictures from a scary story or ghost story you will write. Choose a setting from the box below.

| | | |
|---|---|---|
| China | Vietnam | Mexico |
| Thailand | Cambodia | Eastern Europe |

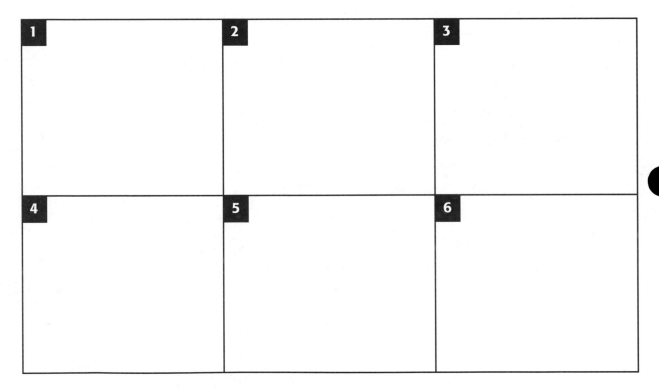

| 1 | 2 | 3 |
|---|---|---|
| | | |
| **4** | **5** | **6** |
| | | |

**B.** ➤ Write a ghost story. Use your storyboard.

_____

_____

_____

_____

_____

_____

# Build Vocabulary

## Find Synonyms

Use with student text page 365.

Words that have similar meanings are called **synonyms.** The words *big* and *huge* are synonyms. Both words mean "large."

➤ Match the underlined word to its synonym.

**Word in a Sentence**

1. _____ Frank lived in a <u>flat</u> before he bought a house.

2. _____ The bricks on his house were <u>crumbling</u> and falling apart.

3. _____ One of the windows was <u>boarded</u> because the glass was broken.

4. _____ Only one person at a time can walk through the <u>tight</u> hallways.

5. _____ Frank parks his car next to the street <u>curb</u> because there is no garage.

6. _____ He wanted to install another <u>washroom</u> for his guests to use.

7. _____ Frank hopes the poor condition of his house is <u>temporary</u>.

**Synonym**

a. close

b. covered

c. apartment

d. bathroom

e. falling apart

f. edge

g. brief

# Writing: Capitalization

Use with student text page 372.

## Capitalize Proper Nouns

**Proper nouns** name specific people, places, and things.
Proper nouns are always capitalized.

We did not always live on **Main Street**.
My friend **Maria** lives in **Texas**.

➤ Rewrite the sentences by correcting the words that should be capitalized.
The first one has been done for you.

1. I wanted to go to simpson street to shop for fabric.

   *I wanted to go to Simpson Street to shop for fabric.*
   _____

2. My friend susan wanted to make clown clothes for our school circus.

   _____

   _____

3. We took the chicago avenue bus to get to the fabric store.

   _____

   _____

4. Our friends josé and mark met us there.

   _____

   _____

5. They are going to enter a clown contest in florida.

   _____

   _____

6. mark told me they won a contest in california last month.

   _____

   _____

# Elements of Literature

*Use with student text page 373.*

## Recognize Point of View in Narratives

Point of view shows us who is telling a story.

| Point of View | | |
|---|---|---|
| **Who Tells the Story** | **What it Means** | **How You Can Tell the Point of View** |
| First Person | A character in the story is the narrator. | Uses *I, me, we, us,* and sometimes *you* |
| Limited Third Person | The narrator is not in the story and does not know what all the characters think and feel. | Uses *he, she,* and *they;* often told from the point of view of one character |
| Omniscient Third Person | The narrator is not in the story and knows what all the characters think and feel. | Uses *he, she,* and *they;* many characters' points of view are given |

➤ Write the point of view of each passage. Use the chart to help you.
Explain what clues support your answer.

Sandra Cisneros and her family moved from one place to another. When they moved to the house on Mango Street, they saw that it needed a lot of work.

1. _____

_____

_____

Sandra was very disappointed to see the new house. She had hoped that it would be shiny and new, or at least freshly painted. At least, she realized, there was a real bathroom for her and the other children.

2. _____

_____

_____

Someday I will have the kind of house I want. I know this is all we can afford right now. But when I get older, I will earn enough money to live in a clean, nice place.

3. _____

_____

_____

# Word Study

*Use with student text page 374.*

## Learn English Words from Other Languages

Many English words come from other languages. Knowing about word origins will help you understand how other languages influence English.

**honest** (Latin): truthful
**desert** (French): a sandy place with little water
**thermos** (Greek): a container that keeps food at a hot or
    cold temperature
**tea** (Chinese): a hot drink made from leaves
**igloo** (Inuit): a house made of ice and snow
**piano** (Italian): a musical instrument with strings, a sounding board,
    and keys
**alligator** (Spanish): a dangerous reptile
**tepee** (Sioux, a native American language): a cone-shaped home made
    of leather or other animal skin

**A.** ➤ Write the language each word comes from.

**1.** igloo     _____

**2.** alligator     _____

**3.** piano     _____

**4.** desert     _____

**B.** ➤ Write a sentence using these words from other languages.

**1. honest**     *Harriet was known to be an honest person who would never tell a lie.*

**2. desert**     _____

**3. thermos**     _____

**4. tea**     _____

**5. igloo**     _____

**6. piano**     _____

**7. alligator**     _____

**8. tepee**     _____

# Grammar Focus

Use with student text page 374.

## Spell Frequently Misspelled Words

The words *there, their,* and *they're* are pronounced the same, but they have different meanings.

**there** a place word, or a word used to say that something exists
**their** possessive form of *they*
**they're** a contraction of "they are"

**A.** ➤ Complete the sentences. Use the correct form of *there, they're,* or *their*.
The first one has been done for you.

1. I promised I would help my little brothers plan _____*their*_____ soccer dinner.

2. _____ so excited about planning this event.

3. It is easy to tell that this is _____ first time planning something this big.

4. _____ is so much to do—shopping, planning a menu, and setting up the tables.

5. Billy wants to put a table near the fireplace, but I told him it would be too warm _____ .

6. _____ going to have to ask some of their friends to help by bringing food.

**B.** ➤ Edit these sentences. Rewrite each sentence using the correct form of *there, they're,* or *their*.

1. There going to the park to play a game of soccer.

_____

2. Pablo and Seth are bringing they're soccer balls.

_____

3. Their will also be a barbecue.

_____

4. The kids will have there parents pick them up after the game.

_____

5. My parents will already be they're.

_____

# Grammar Focus

Use with student text page 374.

## Study Spelling Changes in Noun Plurals

Most plural nouns are formed by adding *-s* to the singular form of the noun. However, some nouns have spelling changes.

| Plural Nouns with Spelling Changes | | |
|---|---|---|
| **Noun** | **Rule** | **Example** |
| singular nouns ending in *f* or *fe* | change the ending to *-ve* before adding *-s* | leaf–leaves<br>life–lives |
| singular nouns ending in *-s*, *-sh*, *-ch*, or *-x* | add *-es* | wish–wishes<br>miss–misses<br>box–boxes |
| singular nouns ending with a consonant + an *-o* | add *-es* | potato–potatoes<br>hero–heroes |

**A.** ➤ Change the singular nouns to plural nouns. Use the chart to help you. The first one has been done for you.

1. wife     _____*wives*_____     5. box     _____

2. tomato     _____     6. beach     _____

3. church     _____     7. shelf     _____

4. thief     _____     8. brush     _____

**B.** ➤ Edit these sentences. Rewrite each sentence using the correct irregular plural form. The first one has been done for you.

1. I need to go to the store to get some tomatos.

    *I need to go to the store to get some tomatoes.* _____

2. In the fall, all the leafes from the trees fall to the ground.

    _____

3. During the flood, there were many heros.

    _____

4. Some people say that cats have nine lifes.

    _____

Student Handbook

5. One of my jobs at home is to wash the dishs after dinner.

    _____

# From Reading to Writing

*Use with student text page 375.*

## Write a Description

When writing a description, it is important to be specific and include details. This will help the reader form a visual image.

Sandra moved to an old house.
Sandra moved to a broken-down house that needed to be painted.

Notice how the second sentence helps form a clearer picture of what the house looks like.

**A.** ➤ Rewrite the paragraph. Be specific and add details to each sentence.

We had a party for my Aunt Anna's birthday. She is old. At the party we ate cake and played some games. We handed out party favors to everyone. Aunt Anna danced, too. The party lasted a long time.

_____

_____

_____

_____

_____

_____

_____

_____

_____

_____

## Across Content Areas

Use with student text page 375.

### Use a Cluster Map

A cluster map can help you organize and create ideas before writing. Read the information below and pay attention to the main idea and details.

Animals make their homes—their *habitats*—in many different places. Some habitats are cold. Others are very wet or hilly. Each animal is comfortable only in certain places.

One example of a habitat is a **cave.** A cave is a hole that is on the side of a mountain. The cave protects the animal from rain and snow. Bears live in caves. Caves can be cold and dark.

Another habitat is the **desert.** The desert is a hot, dry place. There is hardly any rain there. Most of the desert is sand or rock. Animals such as lizards or snakes that do not need much water often live in the desert.

The **jungle** is a place where animals live if they are comfortable in hot places that get a lot of rain. There are many trees and plants in a jungle, and animals such as lions and elephants live there, along with monkeys and birds.

There are very few animals who can stand the coldness of the **tundra.** There are hardly any trees there. Polar bears, seals, and other animals who can survive by eating fish like the tundra.

**A.** ➤ Choose a habitat to write about. Fill in the cluster map. Use the information you just read.

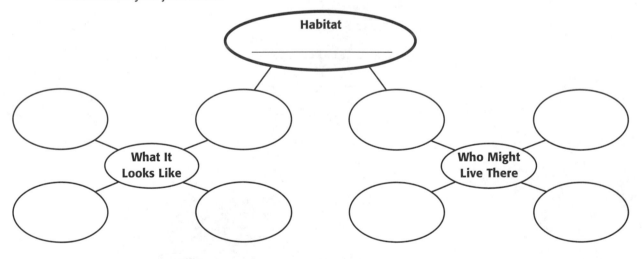

**B.** ➤ Write a short paragraph about the habitat you chose. Use your cluster map to help you.

_____

_____

_____

_____

# Build Vocabulary

**Define Words**

Use with student text page 337.

➤ Complete the sentences. Use the words in the box. The first one has been done for you.

**Word and Definition**

**coated** covered or topped with
**strewn** scattered; spread out in pieces
**clinging** sticking; holding onto tightly
**clusters** clumps or bunches
**flitted** fluttered or darted
**gloating** bragging

1. The butterflies _____*flitted*_____ back and forth.

2. The honey and nuts stick together in _____.

3. The shoes were _____ all over the hallway.

4. The winter storm _____ the ground with fresh snow.

5. She is _____ about winning her prize.

6. The long and stringy plants are _____ to the school walls.

# Writing: Spelling

Use with student text page 388.

## Study Spelling Changes for Words Ending in *y*

A **suffix** is a group of letters added to the end of a word. When a suffix is added to a word that ends in *y*, the spelling of the word may change.

| Spelling Changes in Words Ending in *-y* | | | |
|---|---|---|---|
| **Word Endings** | **Suffixes Added** | **Rules** | **Examples** |
| Consonant + *y* (rely, happy) | Most suffixes (*-ance, -ness*) | Change *y* to *i* | reliance happiness |
| Vowel + *y* (employ, enjoy) | Most suffixes (*-er, -ment*) | Make no change | employer enjoyment |

➤ Write these words with suffixes. Use the chart to help you. The first one has been done for you.

1. _____*heaviness*_____ heavy + *-ness*
2. _____ heavy + *-er*
3. _____ oily + *-ness*
4. _____ oily + *-er*
5. _____ ready + *-ness*
6. _____ steady + *-ness*
7. _____ silly + *-ness*
8. _____ healthy + *–er*
9. _____ dry + *-er*
10. _____ merry + *-ment*
11. _____ pay + *-ment*
12. _____ fly + *-er*
13. _____ enjoy + *-ment*
14. _____ apply + *-ance*
15. _____ foggy + *-ness*
16. _____ defy + *-ance*

# Elements of Literature

Use with student text page 389.

## Understand Problem and Resolution

The **conflict** is the story problem that needs a resolution. It is one part of the plot. The **plot** is the order of events in a story.

**Background** is usually at the beginning. It includes information about the characters and setting. The story problem, or conflict, may be presented in this section.

**Rising action** is when the suspense builds.

**Climax** is the point of greatest suspense in a story. It is the turning point of the action.

**Falling action** is the events that follow the climax.

**Resolution** is when the story comes to a close.

The conflict may be at the beginning or the middle of a story. It may be a problem that a character needs to solve. It may also be a struggle between a character and nature.

**Climax**

**Rising Action**

**Falling Action**

Action and Events

Action and Events

Action and Events

Action and Events

Resolution

Background and Conflict

➤ Fill in the plot diagram for "The Pearl."

**Climax**

**Rising Action**

**Falling Action**

Action and Events

_____

_____

Action and Events

_____

Resolution

_____

Background and Conflict
Write a sentence . . .

_____

_____

# Word Study

Use with student text page 390.

## Learn Words from Latin Roots

Many words in English come from other languages. The word *inspect* means "to look into." It comes from the Latin root *spect*, which means "to look." Knowing the Latin word part will help define other words with *spect*.

Spectator: someone who watches

Spectacles: eyeglasses

Spectacular: something special to see

| Common Latin Roots | | |
|---|---|---|
| **Latin Roots** | **Meanings** | **Examples** |
| **1.** *-cap- (-capt-)* | to take | capable |
| **2.** *-dic- (-dict-)* | to say or point out | dictate |
| **3.** *-fac- (-fact-)* | to do or make | manufacture |
| **4.** *-move- (-mot-)* | to move | motion |
| **5.** *-pon- (-pos-)* | to put or place | position |
| **6.** *-scrib- (-script-)* | to write | script |
| **7.** *-ven- (-vent-)* | to come | invent |
| **8.** *-vert- (-vers-)* | to turn | version |
| **9.** *-vid- (-vis-)* | to see | visual |

➤ Match the words to their meanings. Use the chart to help you.

1. scribble  _____
2. factory  _____
3. capture  _____
4. vision  _____
5. remote  _____
6. posed  _____
7. convention  _____
8. reverse  _____
9. dictionary  _____

a. a gathering that people come to
b. a kind of writing
c. moved far away
d. take and keep
e. a place where things are made
f. a book to find words that people say
g. in one place
h. turn around
i. the ability to see

# Grammar Focus

Use with student text page 390.

## Study Conjunctions

A **compound sentence** is made up of two independent (main) clauses. The two clauses are usually joined by a comma (**,**) and a conjunction.

The **conjunctions** *and, but,* and *or* join two independent (main) clauses in a compound sentence.

| Conjunctions | Rule | Examples |
|---|---|---|
| and | Joins two ideas that are alike | Juana used her paddle, and the canoe moved. |
| but | Joins two ideas that are different | The pearls are pretty, but the shells are bumpy. |
| or | Shows a choice between two ideas | The pearl is inside or the shell is empty. |

➤ Fill in the blanks with *and, but,* or *or.*

1. There were many oysters, _____ some of them had pearls inside.

2. The men looked in the oysters, _____ they didn't find pearls.

3. Did the oyster have a pearl in it, _____ did it have mud?

4. The pearl is beautiful, _____ I can't afford to buy it.

5. Was Kino in the water, _____ was he in the boat?

6. He thought he had an oyster in his hand, _____ it was a rock.

# Grammar Focus

*Use with student text page 390.*

## Review Commas in Compound Sentences

Use a comma (**,**) to join two independent clauses in a compound sentence.

independent clause           independent clause
Sam bought a soccer shirt, **but** he does not play soccer.

**A.** ➤ Edit these sentences. Add the missing commas.

1. Emil is the best student in math but he is not the best student in science.

2. Ivana works at the library and she also works at the school.

3. Tina likes the guitar but she does not like the piano.

4. Does Youssouf speak French at work or does he speak English?

5. When Rosa writes to her cousin, she writes letters or she writes E-mails.

6. Irina calls us in the morning but she does not call us in the evenings.

**B.** ➤ Write compound sentences using the conjunctions *and, but,* and *or* and commas correctly.

1. _____

_____

_____

2. _____

_____

_____

3. _____

_____

_____

4. _____

_____

_____

Student
Handbook

# From Reading to Writing

*Use with student text page 391.*

## Edit a Fiction Story

➤ Use the checklist to edit the fiction story you wrote in Chapter 3

**Editing Checklist for a Fiction Story**

Title of story: _____

**What I did:**

_____ **1.** I included at least two characters.

_____ **2.** I used conjunctions to connect clauses in my story.

_____ **3.** My clauses have subjects and verbs.

_____ **4.** The subjects and verbs in my clauses agree.

_____ **5.** My story has a beginning, a middle, and an end.

_____ **6.** I wrote at least three paragraphs.

_____ **7.** I used reference materials for revising and editing final drafts.

_____ **8.** I used description in my story.

Name _____   Date _____

## Across Content Areas
### Explore Geography

*Use with student text page 391.*

Over 70 percent of the planet Earth is made of water. Much of it is located in the large bodies of water called *oceans*. There are four oceans: the Pacific Ocean, Atlantic Ocean, Indian Ocean, and Arctic Ocean. The great **landforms** or **landmasses** on Earth are the seven continents: Africa, Antarctica, Asia, Australia, Europe, North America, and South America.

An **atlas** is a book with maps. A **globe** is a round object with a world map on it.

➤ Answer as many of the questions as you can. Use an atlas or a globe to check your answers.

1. What three landforms are on the Arctic Ocean?

_____

_____

_____

2. What ocean lies between North America and Europe?

_____

3. What oceans does Australia lie between?

_____

_____

4. Name a landform in the Pacific Ocean.

_____

5. Which two oceans go around Africa?

_____

_____

6. Which two oceans does North America lie between?

_____

_____

# Build Vocabulary

*Use with student text page 393.*

## Understand Context Clues

**Context clues** are the words and sentences that surround a word.

We need to **purify** the environment <u>so we have clean air</u>.

The context clues for *purify* are "so we have clean air." *Purify* means to "clean."

➤ Match the underlined word in each sentence to its definition. Use context clues to help you.

**Word in a Sentence**

1. _____ We have <u>polluted</u> the rivers and streams.

2. _____ Harmful wastes have <u>trashed</u> many natural resources.

3. _____ We may have to travel in ways that we used to, such as the <u>old-fashioned</u> bicycle.

4. _____ Cleaner forms of energy could be <u>produced</u> now.

5. _____ <u>Recycling</u> is a good way to reuse our natural resources.

6. _____ Washing machines, air conditioners, and other home <u>appliances</u> use too much electricity.

7. _____ Small animals can live in plant-filled, watery <u>marshes</u>.

**a.** dirtied

**b** traditional or ancient

**c.** created

**d.** swamps and wetlands

**e.** worn out or ruined

**f.** using things over again

**g.** machines

# Writing: Punctuation

*Use with student text page 400.*

## Punctuate Using Commas in a Series

A **series** is a list of three or more items. Commas are used to separate items in a series.

I have math, science, and social studies homework tonight.

The conjunctions *and* or *or* are used before the last item in the series. Always use a comma before the conjunction that connects the items.

**A.** ➤ Edit these series. Add the missing commas.

1. rivers streams and oceans

2. working playing and raising families

3. fruits grains and vegetables

4. coal oil and gas

5. plants fish snails and bacteria

**B.** ➤ Edit these sentences. Add the missing commas.

1. They will grow fruit grains or vegetables.

2. They travel in cars trucks or trains.

3. Energy will flow from windmills panels and cells.

4. Plants fish and snails purify the water.

5. Our power comes from oil coal or gas.

6. Work food and shopping will change.

# Elements of Literature

*Use with student text page 401.*

## Identify Author's Purpose

The **author's purpose** is the reason that the author writes a text. Purposes for writing are often to entertain, to inform, or to persuade.

**A.** ➤ Read the book topics. Identify the author's main purpose. Write *to entertain, to inform,* or *to persuade.*

1. _____     A book about the history of the state of Texas

2. _____     A speech about the need to recycle to save the environment

3. _____     A fictional adventure story about an explorer sailing the occans

4. _____     A textbook that teaches math concepts and rules

5. _____     A how-to book about building a house

6. _____     A book of poems about animals

**B.** ➤ Write a paragraph about the author's purpose in "What Will Our Towns Look Like?" Use specific examples to support your opinion.

_____

_____

_____

_____

_____

_____

_____

_____

_____

_____

_____

_____

_____

_____

_____

_____

# Word Study

Use with student text page 402.

## Study the Prefix *co-*

A **prefix** is a group of letters added to the beginning of a word.

When a prefix is added to a word, the meaning may change. The prefix *co-* means "together or with." When *co-* is added to the word *author*, the new meaning is "to write with someone else."

**A.** ➤ Read the list of words with the prefix *co-*. Write the definition of each word.

1. cocaptain: _____

2. co-own: _____

3. cofounder: _____

4. cohost: _____

5. colead: _____

**B.** ➤ Complete each sentence with a word with the prefix *co-*. Use context clues to help you.

1. Nicholai is a _____ of the soccer team.

2. Dimitri is a _____ for the party.

3. Mr. Diallo is a _____ of the new medical center.

4. Paulina is going to _____ the play with another actor.

5. Ivan wants to _____ a restaurant with his friend Rachel.

# Grammar Focus

*Use with student text page 402.*

## Use *Will* to Predict Future Events

**Predict** means to tell what might happen in the future.
You can make a prediction by using *will* plus the simple form of a verb.

I *will* finish my homework tonight.

To predict something that you don't think will happen, use *won't*.

I *won't* do very well in the race tomorrow.

**A.** ➤ Unscramble the words and phrases to make predictions. Be sure to use capital letters and periods.

1. will/go/I/after high school/to college _____

2. be/I/won't/late _____

3. interesting/game/be/will/this _____

4. soup/taste/very good/will/this _____

5. won't/our report/we/finish/tonight _____

**B.** ➤ Read these situations and make predictions using *will* plus the simple form of a verb.

1. Cheng is really hungry. He has some money in his pocket. He sees a hotdog stand on the street.

   I think that *Cheng will buy a hotdog and a soda.* _____

2. Fatimah wants to watch a late movie on television. Her parents want her to go to bed because she has a test the next day.

   I think that _____.

3. Tina really likes Ramón. She wants to invite him to go to a party with her. He is walking towards her. He is with another girl.

   I think that _____.

4. My sister and I take the bus to school together every morning. This morning, she got up late. Then it took her forever to get dressed. Now she's making a phone call. Hurry up! Here comes the bus!

   I think that _____.

VISIONS C Activity Book • Copyright © Heinle

VISIONS **Unit 6 • Chapter 4** What Will Our Towns Look Like?

# Grammar Focus

*Use with student text page 402.*

## Contrast Simple Present, Simple Past, and *Will* Future Tenses

The **simple present tense** describes an action that happens regularly or is generally true. The **simple past tense** explains an action that occurred before the present time. The **future tense** using the word *will* predicts an action that will happen in the future or later.

| Simple Present, Simple Past, and Future Tense with *Will* | | |
|---|---|---|
| **Simple Present** | **Simple Past** | **Future with *Will*** |
| I walk. <br> You walk. <br> We walk. <br> They walk. | I walk**ed**. <br> You walk**ed**. <br> We walk**ed**. <br> They walk**ed**. | I *will* walk. <br> You *will* walk. <br> We *will* walk. <br> They *will* walk. |
| He walks. <br> She walks. <br> It walks. | He walk**ed**. <br> She walk**ed**. <br> It walk**ed**. | He *will* walk. <br> She *will* walk. <br> It *will* walk. |

When using the simple present tense, remember to add an *-s* or *-es* to third person singular verbs:

He *watches* television every night.

➤ Complete each sentence with the correct verb form. Look for time clues that tell you when something happens. The first one has been done for you.

1. **pull**    Grace _____*pulled*_____ the candy taffy so it was smooth and wavy.

2. **play**    Tomorrow, I _____ my saxophone for you.

3. **wave**    Yoki _____ at his friends when he rides in the parade next week.

4. **talk**    Pete's brother lives in Atlanta, but he _____ to him a lot.

5. **smile**    Inga _____ for the camera when we took photographs yesterday.

6. **ask**    Pasha did not want to stay late last night, but I _____ her to stay for dinner.

7. **open**    I wonder if the new stores _____ next year.

8. **close**    The old music store _____ its doors last month.

9. **turn**    George _____ his music business over to the new owner soon.

Student Handbook

VISIONS • Unit 6 • Chapter 4 • What Will Our Towns Look Like?

VISIONS C Activity Book • Copyright © Heinle

214

# From Reading to Writing

*Use with student text page 403.*

## Write a Persuasive Letter to the Editor

Write a letter to the editor. Persuade someone reading your letter why the town of the future is a good or bad idea. You can use the information from your interview in Chapter 4.

**A.** ➤ Fill in the chart. Write problems of towns and ways to solve the problems in the future.

| Problems | Solutions to Problems |
|----------|----------------------|
|          |                      |
|          |                      |

**B.** ➤ Write your letter. Use the information in the chart. Provide evidence from the chart to support your opinion.

_____

_____

_____

_____

_____

_____

_____

_____

_____

_____

_____

_____

_____

_____

_____

_____

## Across Content Areas

Use with student text page 403.

### Organize Information in a Chart

➤ Read this information from "What Will Our Towns Look Like?" Each sentence is either a solution to a problem or an example of a problem. Organize the information by filling out the chart.

Factories revolutionized the way we worked, but industrial waste trashed rivers, streams, and oceans.

Electric heat and light made our homes warm and welcoming, but also burned up limited coal and oil.

Cars and trucks will run on clean, hydrogen-powered fuel cells.

We'll often travel on old-fashioned, earth-friendly bicycles.

Since the farms will use natural forms of pest control, there will be far fewer chemicals in the food supply.

The mall will be one big recycling operation.

Our power will come from sources cleaner than coal, oil, and gas.

Some energy will flow from windmills.

Rooftop solar panels will supply electricity.

Plants, fish, snails, and bacteria will naturally purify wastewater.

| Environment Problems and Solutions | | |
|---|---|---|
| **Problem** | **Examples** | **Solutions** |
| Air Pollution | | |
| Water Pollution | | |
| Both | | |